MUSHROOMS

MUSHROOMS

by Michael Chinery

Illustrated by
Bernard Robinson

GRANADA
London Toronto Sydney New York

Granada Publishing Limited
Frogmore, St Albans, Herts AL2 2NF
and
36 Golden Square, London W1R 4AH
515 Madison Avenue, New York, NY 10022, USA
117 York Street, Sydney, NSW 2000, Australia
100 Skyway Avenue, Rexdale, Ontario, M9W 3A6, Canada
61 Beach Road, Auckland, New Zealand

Published by Granada Publishing 1983

British Library Cataloguing in Publication Data

Chinery, Michael
Mushrooms. – (Granada guides; 28)
1. Mushrooms – Juvenile literature
I. Title
589.2′223 QK617

ISBN 0 246 11828 8

Printed and bound in Great Britain by
William Collins Sons & Co Ltd, Glasgow

Contents

Mushrooms and Toadstools

Pin mould (Mucor)is a simple fungus producing spore capsules on its hyphae.

Mushrooms and toadstools belong to the large group of flowerless plants called fungi. They have no leaves and there is never any of the green colour (chlorophyll) found in most other plants. The bulk of the body consists of a mass of fine threads, called hyphae, which spread through or over the food material. This is usually dead plant matter, but it is sometimes living. The threads absorb food from it.

The mushrooms and toadstools that we actually see are just the reproductive parts of the fungi – the fruiting bodies – and they are usually produced only at certain times of the year. They consist of densely packed and entwined hyphae. We normally use the word toadstool for all those fungi with the familiar umbrella-shaped fruiting bodies, but it is often used for other large fungi as well. Mushrooms are basi-

The development of a typical toadstool, from a knot of slender threads to the ripe fruiting body. Growth of the fruiting body is very rapid in damp weather.

Yeast

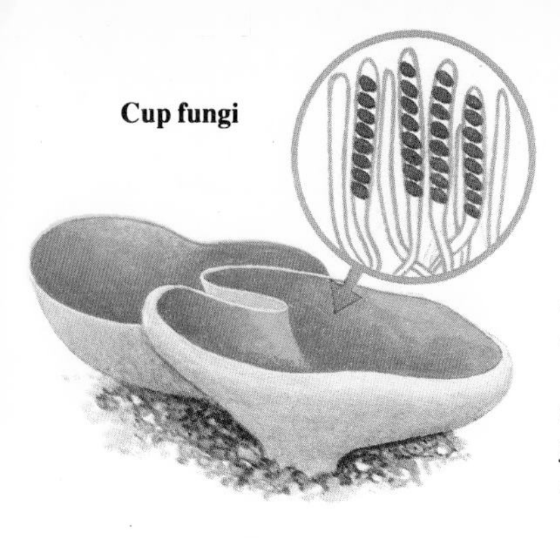

Cup fungi are ascomycetes. The spore-containing asci are embedded in the inner lining, as shown in the enlargement. Yeasts are also ascomycetes; although they produce no fruiting bodies, their spores develop inside other cells.

cally a small group of edible toadstools, but this name is also used in a wider sense for all the umbrella-shaped fungi.

The fruiting bodies do not produce seeds like the flowering plants, but scatter millions of tiny spores, which are usually carried away by the wind. The simplest fungi carry their spores in little capsules on the hyphae and produce no special fruiting bodies.

The larger fungi belong to two major groups – the Ascomycetes and Basidiomycetes. The ascomycetes

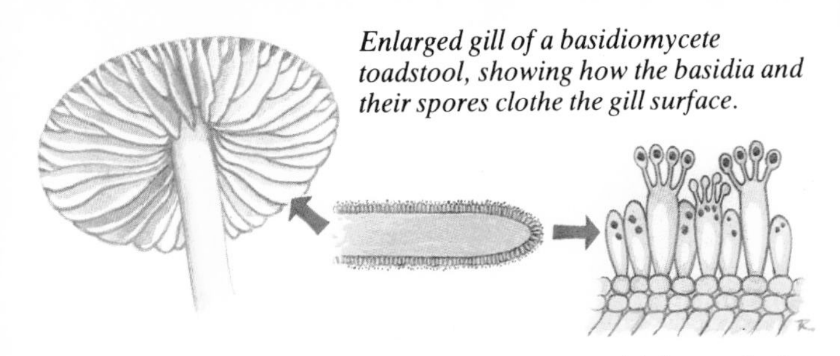
Enlarged gill of a basidiomycete toadstool, showing how the basidia and their spores clothe the gill surface.

form spores *inside* cells called asci, which explode and shoot the spores out when ripe. The cup fungi are the most familiar ascomycetes. All the umbrella-shaped toadstools are basidiomycetes. Their spores develop on the *outside* of club-shaped cells called basidia and they are fired off when ripe.

Fungi are less 'popular' than birds and flowers and only the best known and most conspicuous species acquire English names. These common names are given in this book where they exist, but most of the fungi have only scientific names to identify them.

Most basidiomycete toadstools have gills under the cap. The way in which the gills are attached to the stalk is important in identifying many species.

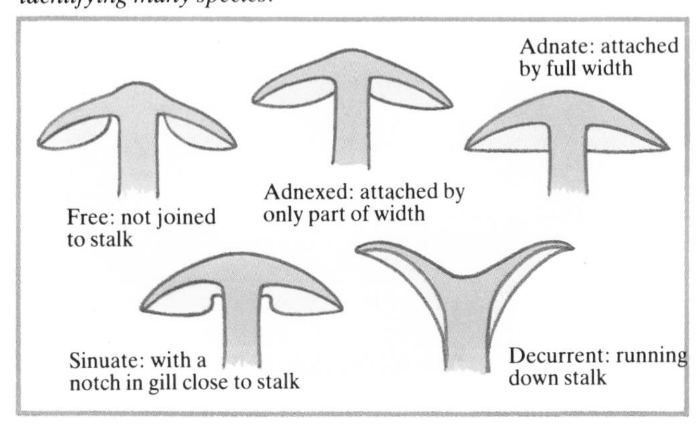

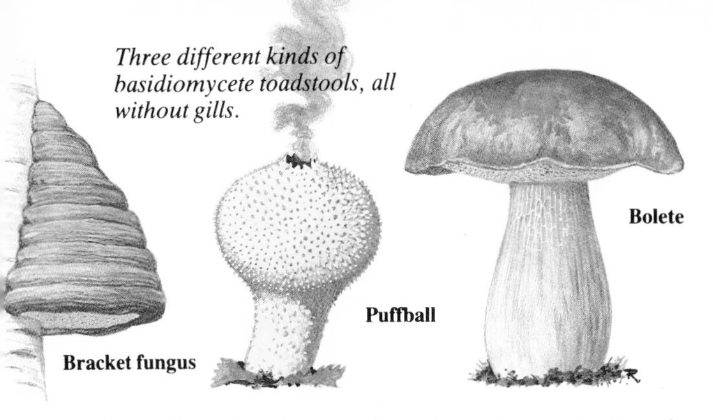

Three different kinds of basidiomycete toadstools, all without gills.

The sizes given for the toadstools at the end of each description are normal maximums for height, followed by the diameter of the cap.

Edible and Poisonous

Many fungi, such as the Chanterelle (page 11) and the Field Mushroom (page 36), are good to eat. But there are also some extremely poisonous species. The Death Cap (page 12) is the most poisonous of all plants and eating only a small portion can be fatal. There is no simple way of separating poisonous ones from edible ones and therefore it is advisable never to eat any wild fungus unless an expert can confirm that it is safe to do so.

Spore colour is important in identifying many gill-bearing toadstools. A spore print can be made by placing a ripe cap on paper for an hour or two.

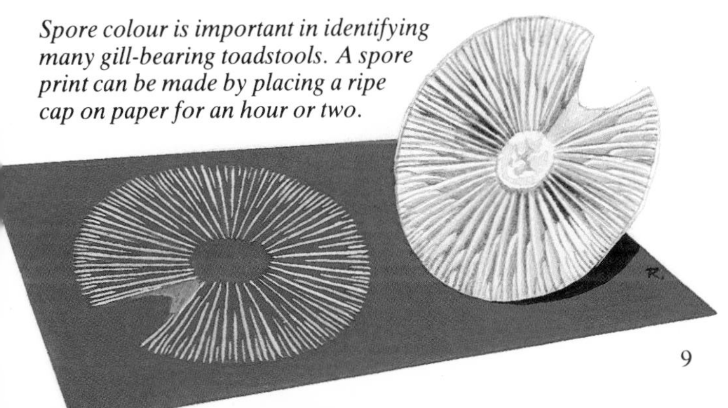

Woodland Toadstools

Woodlands are the best places in which to look for toadstools because there are always plenty of dead leaves and twigs to provide food for them. The fungal threads play a very important part in breaking down the dead leaves and wood and returning their minerals to the soil. The tree roots then take up the minerals again to produce new crops of leaves.

Although most toadstools grow on the ground some prefer tree stumps and fallen trunks or branches. Some actually grow on living trunks. Even those toadstools that spring from the carpet of dead leaves are frequently attached to wood under the ground, their threads often being attached to living tree roots. The great majority of woodland toadstools have radiating gills and belong to the group known as Agarics. Unless otherwise stated, the toadstools shown here grow in all kinds of woodland and appear in the autumn.

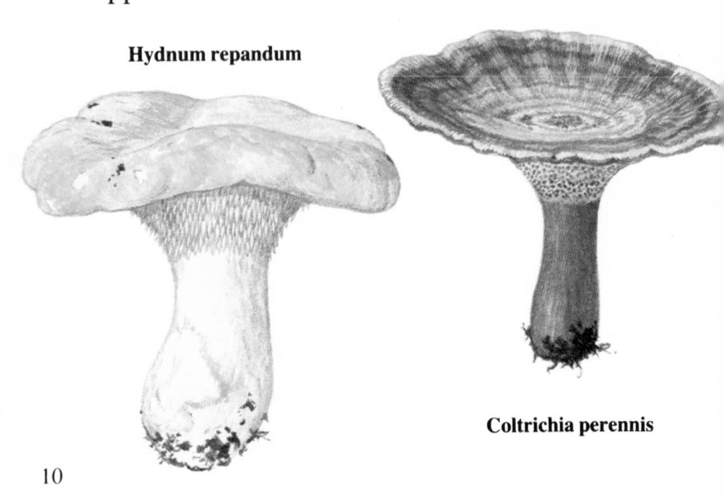

Hydnum repandum

Coltrichia perennis

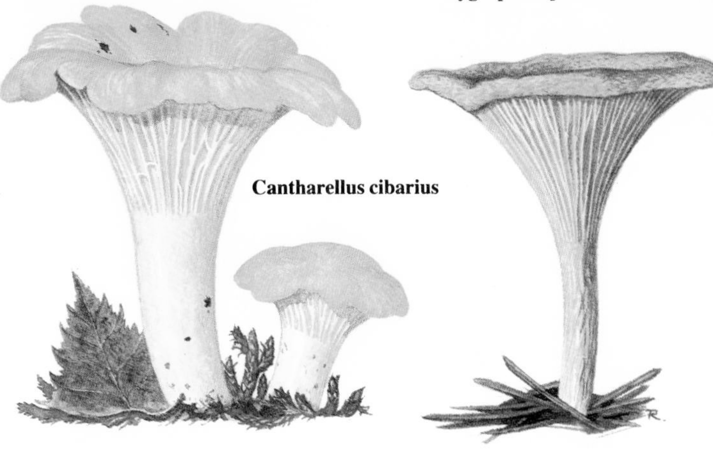

Hydnum repandum is one of a group known as hedgehog fungi. The underside of the cap bears a dense coat of white or pink spines. Deciduous woodlands. Height: 8 cm; cap: 10cm.

Coltrichia perennis is more closely related to the bracket fungi than to other toadstools. The underside of the cap is like a sponge, with a mass of tiny pores. It grows mainly on heathland. Height: 6 cm; cap: 10 cm.

Cantharellus cibarius (**Chanterelle**) is funnel-shaped, although the hollow may be very shallow. It smells of apricots and is good to eat. The outer surface bears a maze of irregularly-branched folds. Deciduous woods. Height: 6 cm; cap: 6 cm.

Hygrophoropsis aurantiaca (**False Chanterelle**) is less fleshy and more orange than the true Chanterelle. It grows mainly in coniferous woods. Height: 6 cm; cap; 6cm.

Craterellus cornucopioides (**Horn of Plenty**) is tubular and has a tough, rubbery texture. Deciduous woods. Height: 12 cm; cap: 8 cm.

Amanita muscaria (Fly Agaric) is a colourful and poisonous toadstool commonly found under birch and pine trees. The white 'warts' on the cap are often missing in older specimens, and the cap may fade to an orange colour. Height: 20 cm; cap: 15 cm.

Amanita phalloides (Death Cap) is extremely poisonous and the deadliest of all the toadstools. It can be recognised by its greenish cap, white gills, a white ring on the stalk, and a ragged bag surrounding the base. Deciduous woodland. Height: 10 cm; cap: 9 cm.

Amanita citrina (False Death Cap) has a much yellower cap, often with patches of white skin on it. There is no bag at the base, but the stalk is swollen like a bulb. It is common in all kinds of woodland. Height: 12 cm; cap: 8 cm.

Amanita fulva (Tawny Grisette) first pushes through the soil like a large, brown

acorn, but the cap soon flattens out. It can usually be recognised by the slightly ribbed margin. Unlike its relatives on this page, the stalk has no ring, but there is a ragged cup or bag at the base. The gills are white. Summer and autumn. Height: 12 cm; cap: 6 cm.

Amanita pantherina is a very poisonous toadstool, recognised by its brown cap clothed with conical white scales. There is a ring near the top of the stalk, and a cup with several ragged collars at the base. The gills are white. It occurs in deciduous woodland, but is not common. Height: 10 cm; cap: 8 cm.

Amanita rubescens (The Blusher) gets its common name because its white flesh turns pink when cut or bruised. There is a ring near the top of the stem, but no cup at the base – just a swollen area with a few scales. The gills are white. Common in late summer and autumn. Height: 12 cm; cap: 12 cm.

Tricholoma sulphureum is easily recognised by its colour and its strong smell of tar. The gills are sinuate and the same colour as the cap. Deciduous woods. Height: 9 cm; cap: 6 cm.

Tricholoma terreum has a soft, felt-like surface to the cap. The gills are white or pale grey, sinuate, and well-separated from each other. It grows mainly in coniferous woods. Height: 8 cm; cap: 6 cm.

Tricholoma ustale has a rather sticky brown cap which gets darker with age. The gills are white at first, but soon become spotted with brown. Deciduous woods. Height: 8 cm; cap: 8 cm.

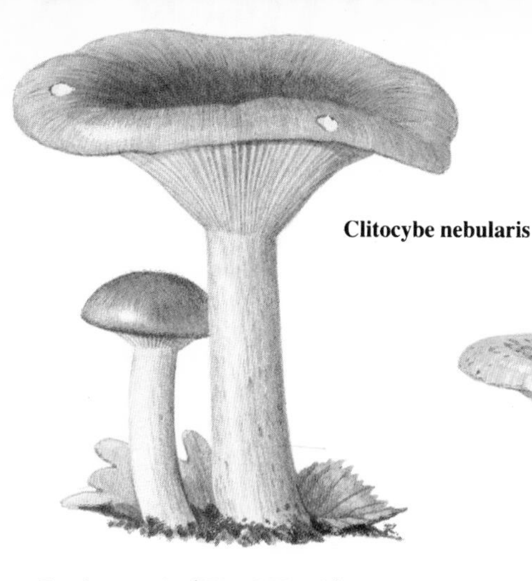

Clitocybe nebularis

Clitocybe flaccida

Lepista nuda (Wood Blewit) varies from chestnut brown to violet and the stalk is violet-blue. The gills are bright violet at first, becoming pink with age. The spores are pink. It grows in deciduous woods and is good to eat. Height: 8 cm; cap: 10 cm.

Clitocybe nebularis is a sturdy toadstool, sometimes tinged with brown. The gills are decurrent (running part-way down the stalk). It often forms large fairy rings and may continue until late in the autumn. It is poisonous. Height: 12 cm; cap: 16 cm.

Clitocybe flaccida has a funnel-shaped cap when mature, with decurrent gills and an in-rolled margin. It is often spotted. It appears in late autumn. Height: 8 cm; cap: 7 cm.

Tricholomopsis rutilans is known as 'plums-and-custard' because of its purplish cap and yellow gills. It grows only on conifer stumps. Height: 10 cm; cap: 12 cm.

Tricholomopsis rutilans

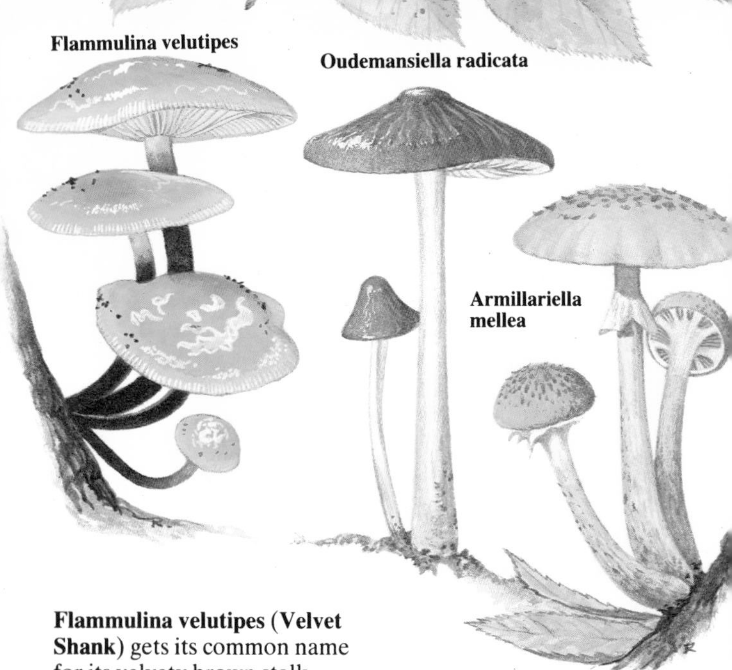

Flammulina velutipes (Velvet Shank) gets its common name for its velvety brown stalk. The cap is rather slimy. The yellowish gills are adnexed and well separated. It grows in large tufts on the stumps and fallen trunks of deciduous trees in late autumn and winter. Height: 6 cm; cap: 5 cm.

Oudemansiella radicata has a rather sticky cap, especially when wet. Its tough, slender stalk is prolonged into an underground 'root' as much as 30 cm long. This springs from buried wood or roots. It grows in deciduous woods in summer and autumn. Height: 18 cm; cap: 8 cm.

Armillariella mellea (Honey Fungus) is a common toadstool, appearing in tufts at the bases of trees. It often kills the trees, and then goes on living on the dead trunks. The ring is thick and often spotted with yellow. Height: 15 cm; cap; 12 cm.

Laccaria laccata (The Deceiver) gets its common name because it occurs in so many forms. The gills are large and flesh-coloured, with a waxy texture. The stalk is often twisted. Common in all kinds of woods and on heaths. Height: 6 cm; cap: 4 cm.

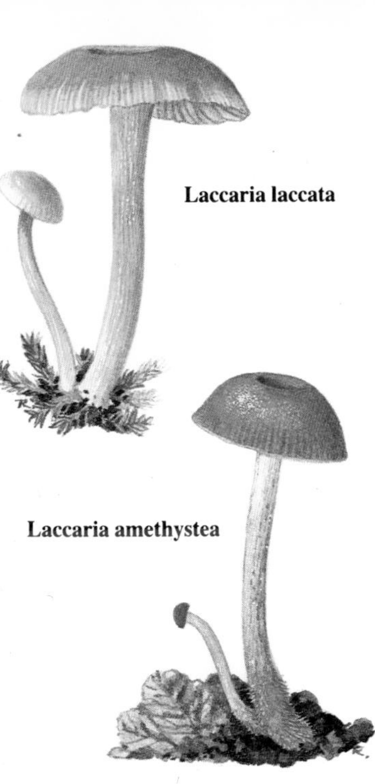

Laccaria amethystea (Amethyst Deceiver) is easily recognised by its colour and its well-separated gills. It is common in deciduous woodland. Height: 7 cm; cap: 4 cm.

Collybia peronata (Wood Woolly Foot) gets its common name for the woolly base of its stalk. The whole toadstool is very leathery and does not snap like most fungi. It is very common in leaf litter in deciduous woodlands. Height: 10 cm; cap: 6 cm.

Collybia fusipes (Spindle Shank) is a tufted toadstool with a tough, grooved stalk that becomes very narrow at the base. It grows at the bases of tree trunks in summer and autumn. Height: 10 cm; cap: 7 cm.

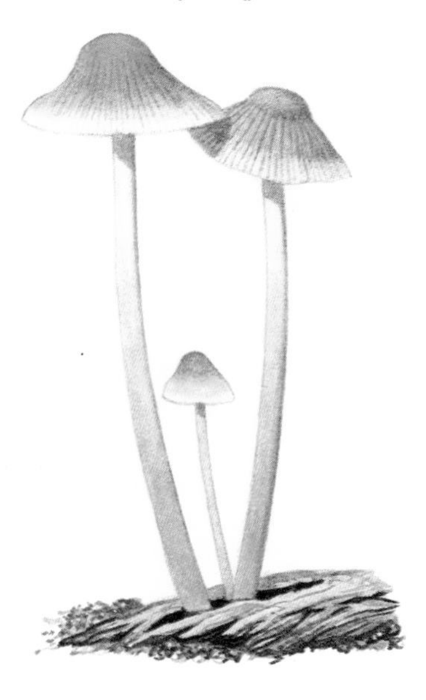

Mycena galericulata has a bell-shaped and rather leathery cap varying from pale brown to grey. The margins are streaked or slightly grooved. The stalk is tough and shiny. The gills are widely spaced, white at first and then flesh-coloured. It grows in clumps on tree stumps and buried wood. Height: 10 cm; cap: 5 cm.

Mycena galopus is very brittle. Its stalk exudes a white juice when broken. The cap is bell-shaped with a dark centre and a grooved margin. The gills are white. It is very common in woods and hedgerows. Height: 5 cm; cap: 1 cm.

Mycena vitilis has a prominent central point on its grey or brownish cap. The stalk is

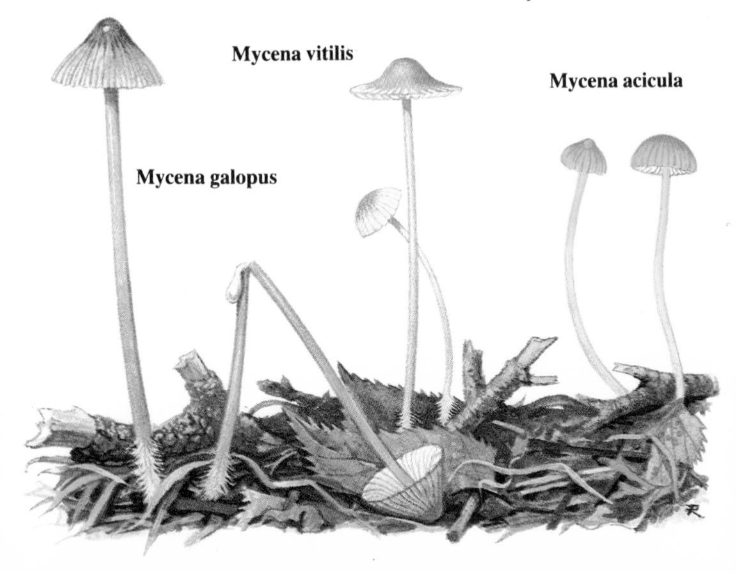

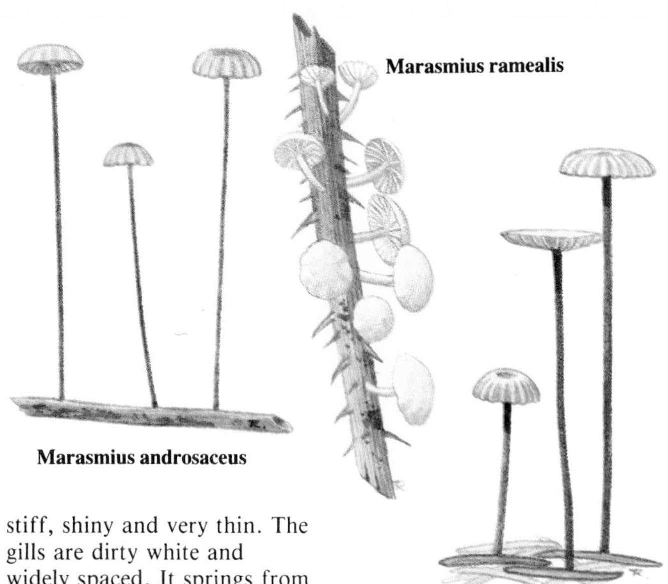

Marasmius perforans

stiff, shiny and very thin. The gills are dirty white and widely spaced. It springs from dead twigs in deciduous woods in summer and autumn. Usually solitary. Height: 8cm; cap: 1.5cm.

Mycena acicula (Orange Bonnet) grows on rotting twigs and other pieces of wood and can be found from spring until autumn. The gills are yellow. Height; 4 cm; cap: 1 cm.

Marasmius androsaceus (Horse-hair Fungus) has a very slender shiny black stalk resembling a horse hair. The threads also resemble matted black horse hair. The cap is brown and wrinkled; gills are brown. It grows on conifer needles and small twigs, especially heather, in summer. Height: 6 cm; cap: 7 cm.

Marasmius ramealis ranges from dirty white to flesh-coloured. The cap is flat and wrinkled and the stalk is usually strongly curved. Gills are white. It grows on dead twigs, especially bramble, in summer and autumn. Height: 2 cm; cap: 1 cm.

Marasmius perforans has a thin velvety black stalk and a wrinkled, flesh-coloured cap. The gills are off-white and widely spaced. The whole fungus has an unpleasant smell. It grows on dead conifer needles. Height: 4 cm; cap: 1.5 cm.

Psathyrella gracilis

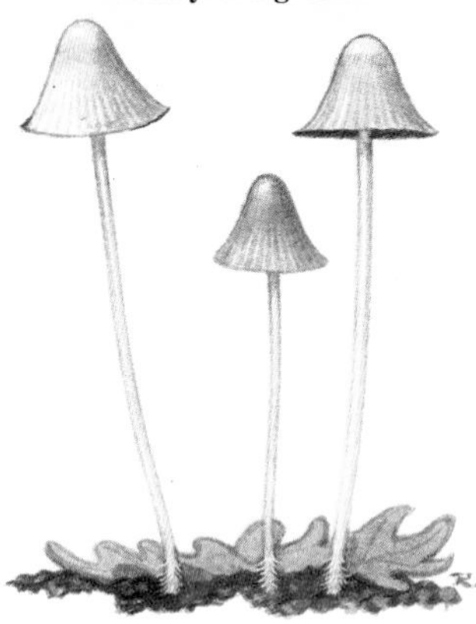

Psathyrella gracilis is a fragile toadstool with a brown bell-shaped cap and dark gills with pink edges. Abundant in woodlands, it also grows in hedgerows and on roadsides. Height: 10 cm; cap 2.5 cm.

Coprinus disseminatus (**Crumble Cap**) is another fragile species, often found in thousands on rotten logs and tree stumps. The gills are grey or black without pink edging. It occurs mainly in autumn. Height: 5 cm; cap: 1 cm.

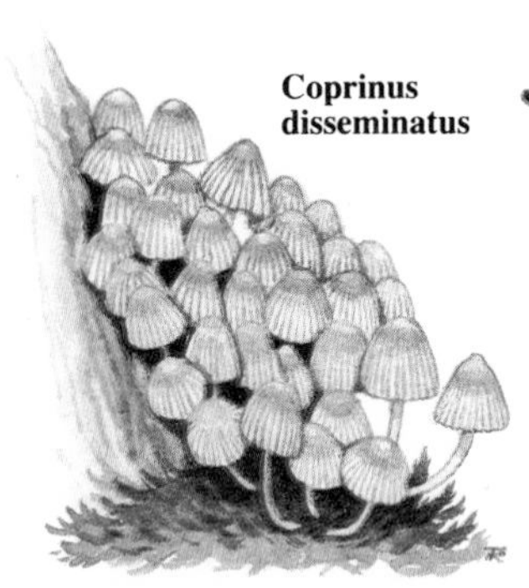

Coprinus disseminatus

Coprinus micaceus

Coprinus micaceus is a larger and darker relative of the Crumble Cap. The cap is dotted with shiny flakes at first, but these fall as the cap opens out. The edges become ragged as a result of auto-digestion (see Ink Cap, page 37). It grows on deciduous stumps from spring to late autumn. Height: 10 cm; cap: 5 cm.

Galerina mutabilis

Galerina mutabilis has a brown cap when moist, but the central region is much paler when dry. The lower part of the stalk (below the ring) bears many pointed scales. It grows on deciduous tree stumps. Height: 6 cm; cap: 3 cm.

Pholiota squarrosa is easily recognised by its coat of bristly scales. The gills are yellowish at first and then rust-coloured.

Hypholoma fasciculare

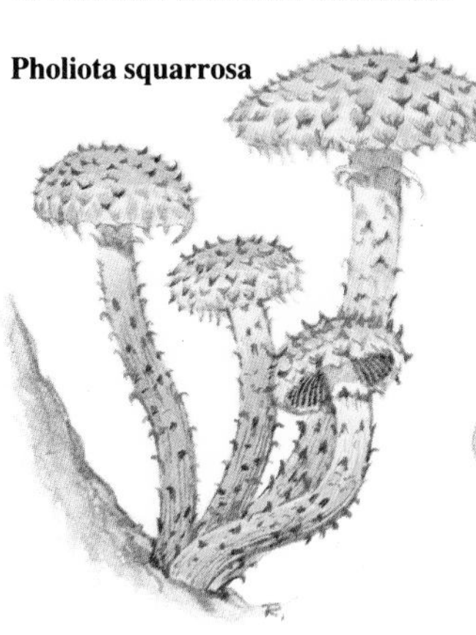

Pholiota squarrosa

It forms dense tufts at the bases of living deciduous trees. Height: 10 cm; cap: 8 cm.

Hypholoma fasciculare (Sulphur Tuft) grows in clumps on the bases of tree stumps. It is very common, especially in autumn. The gills are sinuate, yellow at first and then olive-green.
Height: 8 cm; cap: 4 cm.

Hypholoma sublateritium

Hypholoma sublateritium is a brick-coloured or orange relative of Sulphur Tuft. The gills are yellow at first but become purplish or violet-brown with age. It grows like Sulphur Tuft.
Height: 10 cm; cap: 8 cm.

Agaricus xanthodermus

Agaricus silvicola

Agaricus silvicola (Wood Mushroom) has a swollen, bulb-like base to the stalk and a droopy ring which is sometimes double. The cap and stalk become yellow with age, but not brightly so. Gills are greyish-white at first and then brownish. Spores are chocolate brown.
Height: 12 cm; cap: 12 cm.

Agaricus xanthodermus (Yellow-staining Mushroom) resembles the previous species, but the cap and stalk, especially at the base, turn bright yellow when cut. It is poisonous. The gills are white at first and then purplish-brown. Spores are purplish-brown. Woods and shrubby places. Height: 8 cm; cap: 8 cm.

Inocybe geophylla has a more or less bell-shaped cap with a silky surface. It is poisonous. The gills are adnexed, white at first and then greyish-brown. Deciduous woods.
Height: 4 cm; cap: 2.5 cm.

Inocybe geophylla

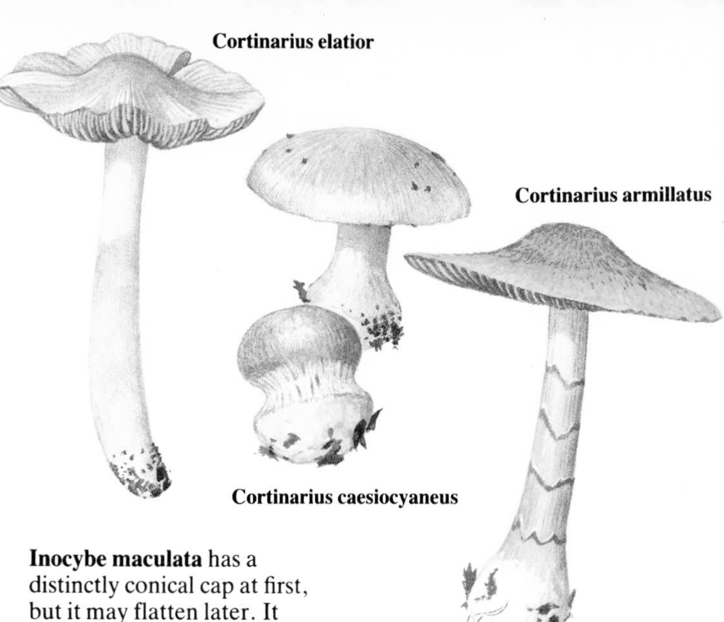

Inocybe maculata has a distinctly conical cap at first, but it may flatten later. It bears many light and dark scales, and is poisonous. Paths and clearings in deciduous woods. Height: 10 cm; cap: 7 cm.

Cortinarius elatior is light brown or olive-brown and, like all species of *Cortinarius*, it has cobweb-like strands around the gills when young. Gills are rusty brown. Deciduous woods, especially beech. Height: 8 cm; cap: 2 cm.

Cortinarius caesiocyaneus is blue when young but turns brown with age. The cap is sticky. The stalk has a platform-like base. The gills are bluish-violet at first and then brown. Beech woods. Height: 8 cm; cap: 10 cm.

Cortinarius armillatus is easily recognised by the red bands on the stalk. The cap ranges from tan to deep brick colour. Gills are rusty brown. With birch trees in woods and on heaths. Height: 12 cm; cap: 10 cm.

Paxillus involutus

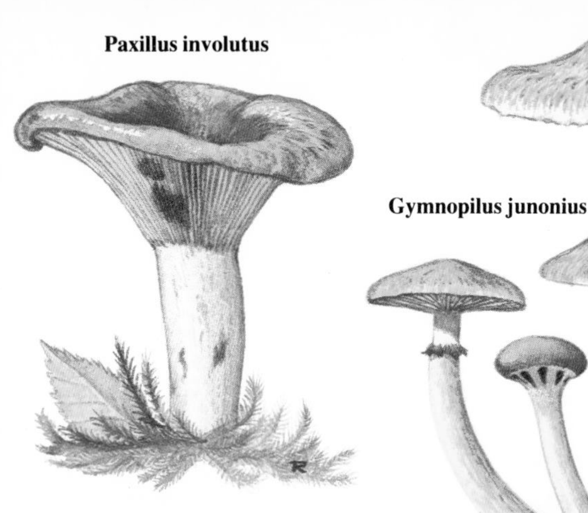

Gymnopilus junonius

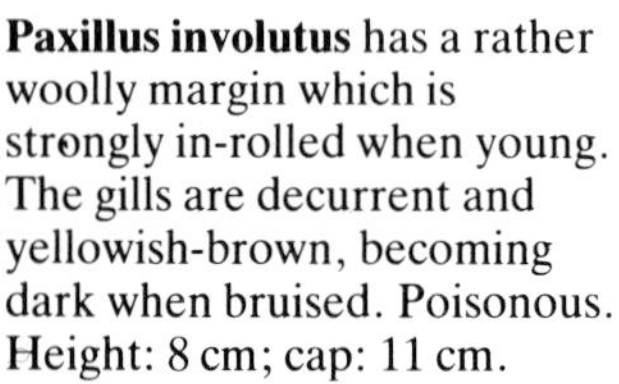

Paxillus involutus has a rather woolly margin which is strongly in-rolled when young. The gills are decurrent and yellowish-brown, becoming dark when bruised. Poisonous. Height: 8 cm; cap: 11 cm.

Gymnopilus junonius forms dense tufts on the bases of living and dead deciduous trees. The cap is distinctly scaly. The gills are adnate and yellow to rust-coloured. Height: 15 cm; cap: 12 cm.

Lactarius tabidus

Milky Mushrooms

Lactarius species are flat or funnel-shaped, with slightly decurrent gills. All exude milky droplets when the gills are broken. The taste of this milk is important in identifying the species.

Lactarius tabidus has mild white milk which becomes yellow when it dries on a tissue. Gills are pale buff. Common in deciduous woods. Height: 4 cm; cap: 4 cm.

Lactarius turpis (The Ugly One) has a sticky surface and a felty, in-rolled margin. Milk is

Lactarius turpis

white and very peppery. Under birches. Height: 10 cm; cap: 20 cm.

Lactarius rufus has a distinct central nipple. Gills are yellow to flesh-coloured. Milk is white and very peppery after a short while. Coniferous woods. Height: 8 cm; cap: 6 cm.

Lactarius deliciosus has a variable amount of green staining on the cap. The gills also turn green when damaged. Milk is carrot-coloured. Coniferous woods. Height: 10 cm; cap: 10 cm.

Lactarius piperatus has a smooth white cap and densely crowded white gills with peppery white milk. Deciduous woods. Height: 10 cm; cap: 15 cm.

Lactarius rufus

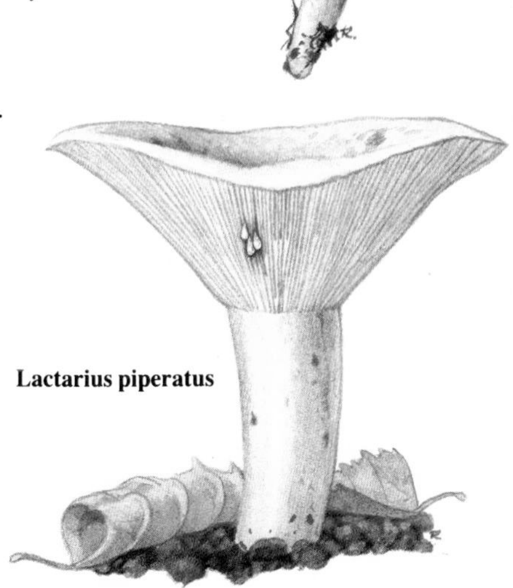

Lactarius piperatus

Lactarius deliciosus

Brittle Gills

The toadstools on these two pages are known as Brittle Gills, for the gills break very easily. The toadstools are usually strongly domed at first but they flatten out and often become funnel-shaped. Most species have no short gills in the outer part of the cap.

Russula emetica

Russula nigricans

Russula emetica (The Sickener) has a scarlet cap and a pure white stalk. The gills are adnexed and pure white. It is poisonous. Coniferous woods. Height: 8 cm; cap: 7 cm.

Russula nigricans is pale brown at first but blackens with age. The gills are adnate and widely spaced and there are short gills around the margin. The flesh is white, but reddens shortly after cutting. Deciduous woods. Height: 8 cm; cap: 7 cm.

Russula delica is flat from the start, white at first but becoming yellowish and often spotted with brown. Gills are slightly decurrent, often with a bluish tinge at the base. There are some short gills near the margin. Height: 10 cm; cap: 15 cm.

Russula fellea smells of geraniums. It has a waxy cap and adnexed, honey-coloured gills. Deciduous woods. Height: 7 cm; cap: 9 cm.

Russula delica

Russula ochroleuca resembles *fellea* but its cap is brighter yellow and its gills are white. It has no smell. Height: 10 cm; cap: 9 cm.

Russula cyanoxantha ranges from bluish-green to violet. The gills are white and greasy and less brittle than in other *Russula* species. Deciduous woods in summer and autumn. Height: 12 cm; cap: 10 cm.

Russula atropurpurea ranges from purplish-red to almost black, often with yellow mottling when old. The gills are adnexed and white, often with rusty spots. Common in deciduous woods in summer and autumn. Height: 8 cm; cap: 10 cm.

Russula xerampelina is usually purple or brownish-red; occasionally it is olive green, with reddish veins on the stalk. Gills are cream or straw-coloured. It smells of crabs. Late summer and autumn. Height: 10 cm; cap: 12 cm.

Boletes

These are toadstools in which the underside of the cap is sponge-like, with masses of tiny pores instead of gills. Unlike the Bracket Fungi (page 42), the spongy part is easily detached from the rest of the cap. Several species are very good to eat. Only the Devil's Boletus (page 30) is poisonous. They all grow on the ground.

Suillus luteus, like all members of its genus, has a sticky cap when moist. The ring is well developed. It grows in coniferous woods.
Height: 10 cm; cap: 12 cm.

Suillus bovinus has no ring. The pores are large and usually sub-divided. The flesh is yellow to reddish. Coniferous woods.
Height: 8 cm; cap: 7 cm.

Suillus grevillei has bright yellow pores and yellow flesh. The ring disappears with age. Spores are yellowish. It always grows with larch.
Height: 10 cm; cap: 9 cm.

Suillus granulatus has no ring. The pores are yellow at first, turning brown with age. They ooze milky drops when young. Under conifers.
Height: 10 cm; cap: 10 cm.

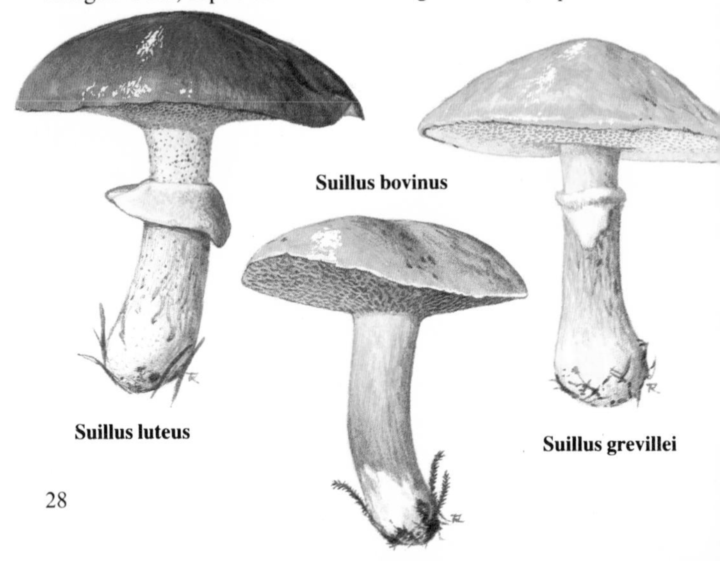

Suillus bovinus

Suillus luteus

Suillus grevillei

Suillus variegatus has many dark scales on the cap. There is no ring. The pores are small and brown, becoming bluish when bruised. It grows under conifers. Height: 8 cm; cap: 12 cm.

Boletus subtomentosus, like all *Boletus* species, has no ring. The cap sometimes cracks and the yellowish flesh shows through. The pores are very coarse and golden yellow, becoming blue when bruised. Deciduous woods and in heathland. Height: 10 cm; cap: 10 cm.

Boletus badius is shiny when dry and slightly slimy when wet. The pores are pale yellow, but turn blue-green when bruised. Height: 8 cm; cap: 10 cm.

Suillus variegatus

Suillus granulatus

Boletus badius

Boletus subtomentosus

Boletus chrysenteron

Boletus chrysenteron is easily recognised by its pinkish-brown cap which splits to reveal pink flesh below. The yellowish pores are large and angular. It is common in deciduous woods.
Height: 9 cm; cap: 7 cm.

Boletus erythropus has a very dark brown or reddish-brown cap and blood-red pores. The stalk bears red spots. The flesh is yellow, but all parts immediately turn blue when bruised. Deciduous woods.
Height: 12 cm; cap: 11 cm.

Boletus satanas (Devil's Boletus) is poisonous. It can be recognised by its pale cap, blood-red pores, and the red network on the greatly swollen stalk. Flesh is yellow, turning slightly blue in upper regions when damaged. Beechwoods.
Height: 12 cm; cap: 18 cm.

Boletus edulis is one of the best of all edible fungi. It is recognised by its bun-like cap, pale pores, and the white network on the stem. Spores are yellowish.
Height: 15 cm; cap: 20 cm.

Boletus satanas

Boletus erythropus

Boletus felleus can be recognised by its angular pink pores under the yellowish-brown cap. There is a dark network on the stalk. Spores are pink. It grows mainly in coniferous woods.
Height; 10 cm; cap: 12 cm.

Leccinum scabrum has a dry cap and a rough stalk. The pores are greyish-brown and tiny, and the flesh is white. It grows with birch trees in woods and on heaths.
Height: 15 cm; cap: 10 cm.

Leccinum versipelle also grows with birches, but is easily distinguished from the previous species by its orange cap. The flesh is white at first, but darkens with age.
Height: 15 cm; cap: 13 cm.

Grassland Toadstools

Many gill-bearing toadstools grow in fields and meadows, nourished by the decaying roots and leaves of the grasses. They are especially common where animals graze, for the dung adds to the food supply. The toadstools often grow in 'fairy rings'. These develop because the fungal threads gradually exhaust the food supply in the centre of a patch. The threads die there, leaving just a ring round the outside. The threads continue to spread outwards, and so the ring gradually gets larger. They cannot spread back to the middle because the food has been exhausted inside the ring.

Hygrophorus conicus has a distinctly conical cap with a prominent central point. It is red or yellow but blackens with age. All parts of the toadstool turn black when bruised. Summer and autumn. Height: 6 cm; cap: 5 cm.

Hygrophorus obrusseus starts off with a conical cap but soon flattens out. It is slimy when wet. The gills are free and, as in all *Hygrophorus* species, are thick, widely-spaced, and waxy. Summer and autumn. Height: 10 cm; cap: 8 cm.

Hygrophorus pratensis has a bell-shaped cap at first but it soon flattens out and becomes top-shaped. The widely-spaced decurrent gills and the pale tan colour make this

Hygrophorus obrusseus

Hygrophorus conicus

toadstool quite easy to recognise. Late summer till winter. Height: 8 cm; cap: 6 cm.

Hygrophorus puniceus has a bright red cap at first, but it becomes yellowish with age. It is always conical or pyramidal, often lop-sided, but never flat. The yellow or orange gills are adnexed, with a waxy texture. Late summer to winter. Height: 10 cm; cap: 10 cm.

Clitocybe rivulosa is a very poisonous toadstool often forming fairy rings on lawns and other areas of short grass. The cap is flat and flesh-coloured, with an in-rolled margin and a slight hollow in the centre. It is powdery when young. The gills are densely packed and slightly decurrent. The stalk is often twisted. Late summer and autumn. Height: 5 cm; cap: 5 cm.

Clitocybe rivulosa

Hygrophorus puniceus

Hygrophorus pratensis

Tricholoma gambosum (St George's Mushroom) has a smooth cap, white at the edge and pale buff in the centre. The gills are sinuate and white. It is good to eat. Spring. Height: 8 cm; cap: 10 cm.

Lepista saeva (Blewit) ranges from pale tan to grey. The stalk is violet, the gills are white to flesh-coloured and spores are pale pink. It often forms fairy rings and is good to eat. Autumn and early winter. Height: 8 cm; cap: 8 cm.

Mycena flavo-alba grows in short grass and is common on lawns. It is usually tinged with yellow in the centre. Gills are white, adnate at first but then free. Late summer and autumn. Height: 3 cm; cap: 2 cm.

Mycena fibula (The Carpet Pin) has a thin cap and is very fragile. The gills are yellowish-brown and strongly decurrent. Damp grassy places in summer and autumn. Height: 4 cm; cap: 2 cm.

Marasmius oreades is the commonest fairy-ring toadstool on lawns and verges, although it does not always form rings. The gills are adnexed and widely-spaced. Late summer and autumn. Height: 7 cm; cap: 5 cm.

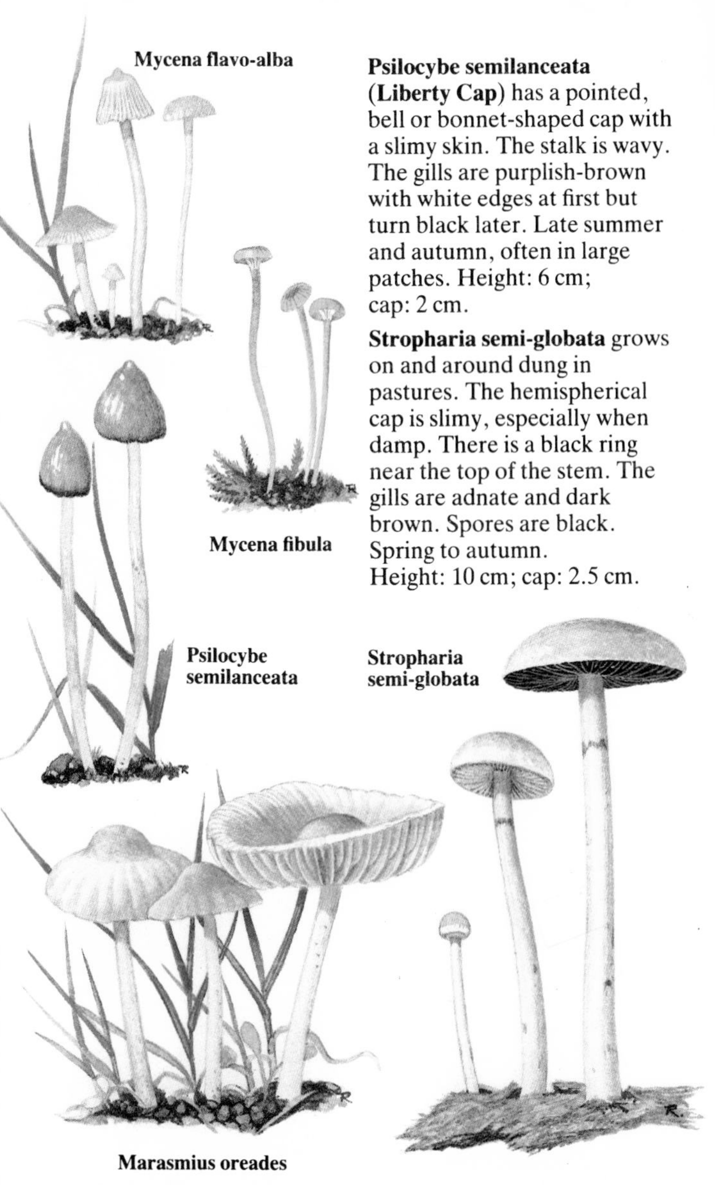

Psilocybe semilanceata (Liberty Cap) has a pointed, bell or bonnet-shaped cap with a slimy skin. The stalk is wavy. The gills are purplish-brown with white edges at first but turn black later. Late summer and autumn, often in large patches. Height: 6 cm; cap: 2 cm.

Stropharia semi-globata grows on and around dung in pastures. The hemispherical cap is slimy, especially when damp. There is a black ring near the top of the stem. The gills are adnate and dark brown. Spores are black. Spring to autumn. Height: 10 cm; cap: 2.5 cm.

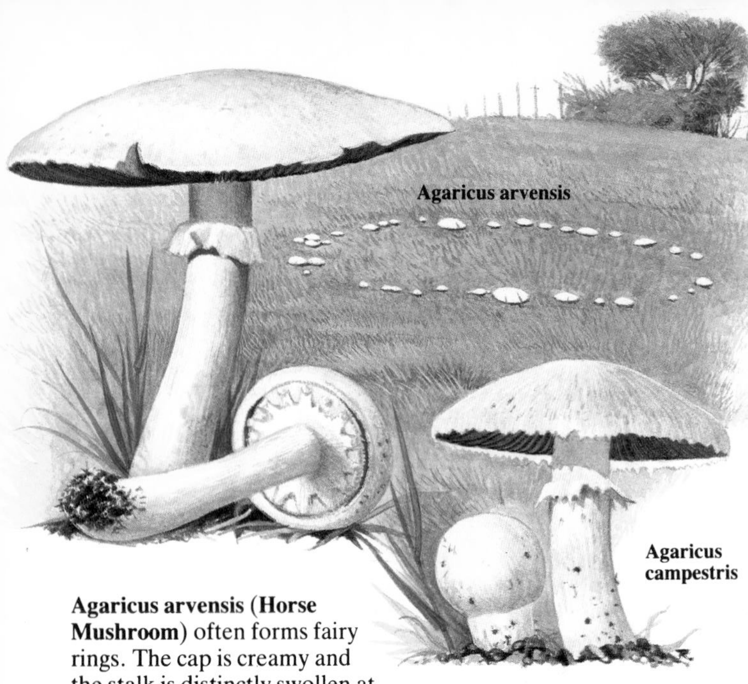

Agaricus arvensis (Horse Mushroom) often forms fairy rings. The cap is creamy and the stalk is distinctly swollen at the base. There is a ring on the stem and in the young stages it resembles a cogwheel just under the gills. The gills are white at first and then purplish-brown: never pink. It is very good to eat. Spores are purplish-brown. Autumn. Height: 15 cm; cap: 12 cm.

Agaricus campestris (Field Mushroom) is the common mushroom that people gather in the fields. The stalk is not swollen at the base. The gills are pink at first and then purplish-brown. Spores are purplish-brown. The flesh is white but may turn pink on cutting. It is excellent to eat. Height: 6 cm; cap: 8 cm.

Lepiota procera (Parasol Mushroom) is easily recognised by its scaly cap with a central nipple and by the wavy pattern on the stalk. The flesh and gills are white. It is very good to eat. Summer and autumn, often near trees. Height: 25 cm; cap: 15 cm.

Lepiota rhacodes (Shaggy Parasol) is similar to *L. procera* but has no nipple and no wavy markings on the stalk. Its flesh reddens slightly when broken.

Coprinus comatus (Shaggy Ink Cap) is readily identified by its shape and shaggy cap. The gills are pink when young but

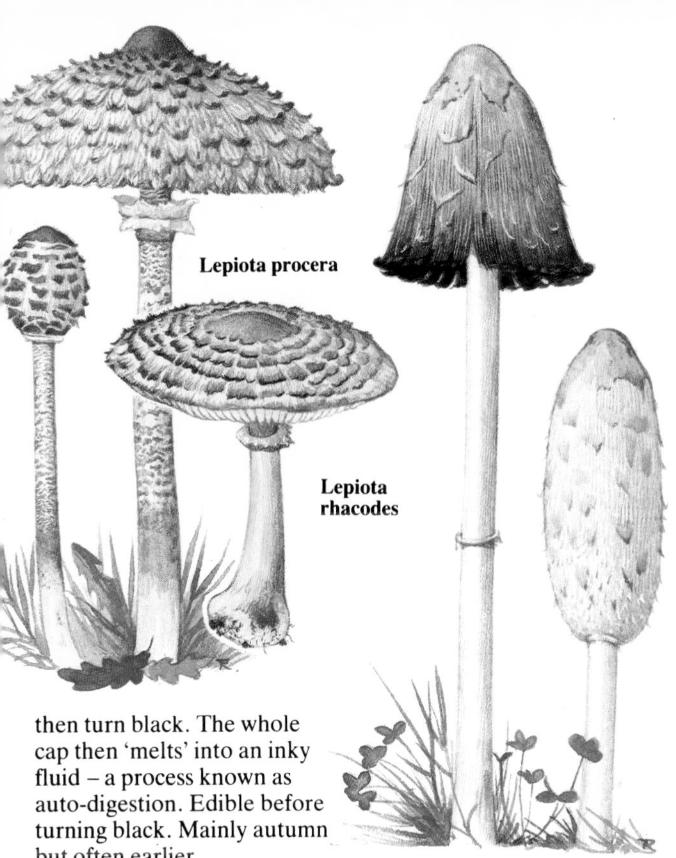

Lepiota procera

Lepiota rhacodes

Coprinus comatus

then turn black. The whole cap then 'melts' into an inky fluid – a process known as auto-digestion. Edible before turning black. Mainly autumn but often earlier.
Height: up to 30 cm.

Coprinus plicatilis is acorn-shaped at first but then opens to form a delicate umbrella. The cap is very thin and ridges mark the positions of the gills underneath. The gills are black but do not liquefy as in most *Coprinus* species. Damp grassy places in autumn, usually growing singly. Height: 8 cm; cap: 3 cm.

Coprinus plicatilis

Puffballs and Relatives

This group of fungi includes the stinkhorns and the bird's nest fungi as well as the puffballs and earth-stars. They are basidiomycetes in which the spores develop inside a completely closed fruiting body. The latter splits open when ripe and the spores can then escape. A leaf or a rain-drop falling on to a ripe puffball or earth-star causes it to puff out a little cloud of spores.

Phallus impudicus (Stinkhorn) grows in woods in summer and autumn. Starting as a small 'egg', it grows to about the size of a golf ball and then splits open. The spongy stalk grows up from the 'egg'. Its cap is covered with foul-smelling, brownish slime containing millions of spores. You will smell a stinkhorn long before you see it. Flies come to feed on the slime, and they pick up the spores and carry them away. Height: 15 cm. The smaller and less smelly **Mutinus caninus (Dog Stinkhorn)** grows in woods in the autumn.

Langermannia gigantea (Giant Puffball) grows in woods and grassland in autumn. It is attached to the ground by a

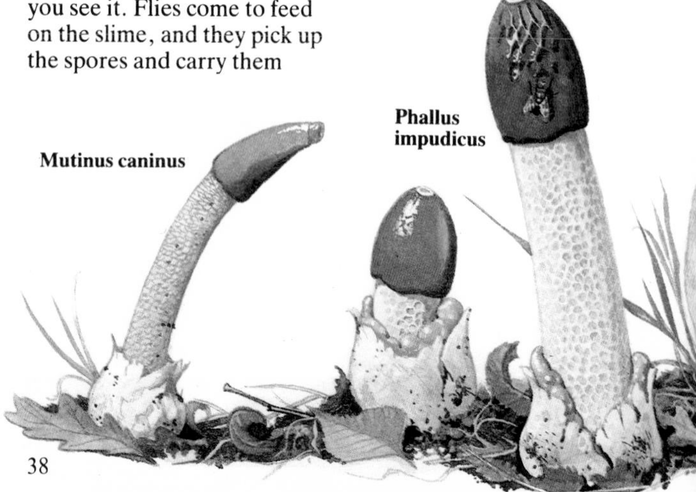

slender thread. The soft, suede-like skin flakes away when ripe to reveal the mass of dark spores. Up to 30 cm across.

Calvatia excipuliformis grows in woods and grasslands in autumn. The skin flakes away at the top when ripe, leaving just a small hole for the spores to escape. Height: 15 cm.

Bovista nigrescens is a grassland puffball appearing in autumn. It is white at first but becomes black and papery when ripe. It has a wide opening with a distinct rim. It often breaks free from the ground and rolls along in the wind, scattering spores as it goes. Up to 6 cm across.

Vascellum pratense

Vascellum pratense is common in grassy places in summer and autumn. Rather knobbly at first, it becomes smooth and brown as it ripens. It splits at the top to allow the spores to escape in the breeze. Up to 4 cm across.

Calvatia excipuliformis

Langermannia gigantea

Bovista nigrescens

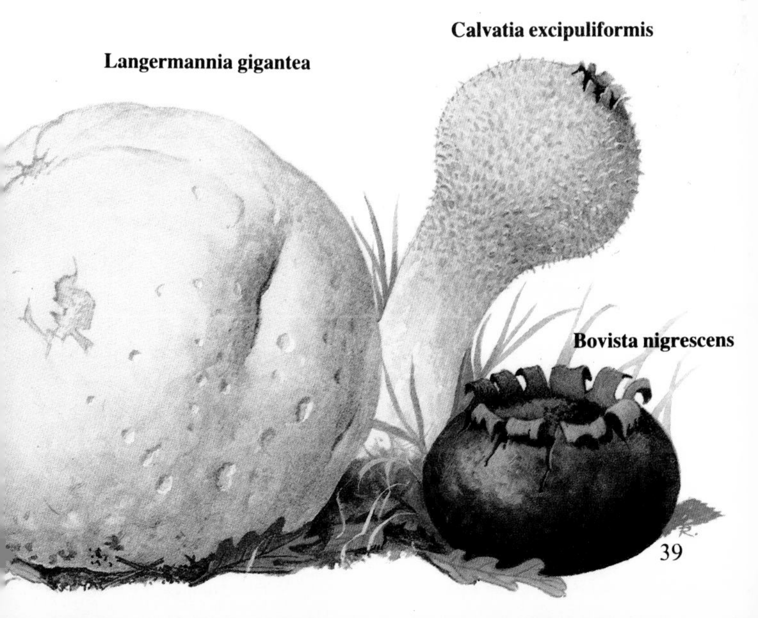

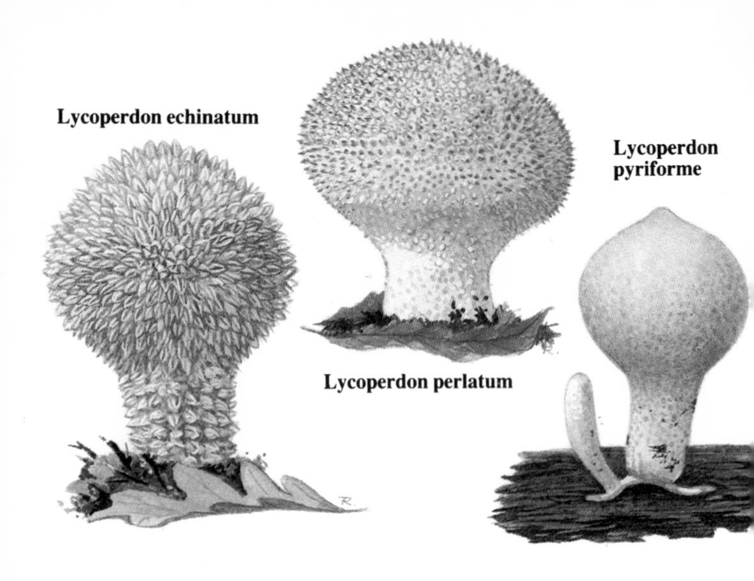

Lycoperdon echinatum is a woodland puffball. It is very spiny at first, but the spines fall as it ripens, leaving a netted pattern on the skin. Like other Lycoperdon species, it appears in autumn and the spores escape through a small hole at the top. About 6 cm across.

Lycoperdon perlatum is very common. It has a distinct stalk and is covered with 'warts' when young. Up to 5 cm across.

Lycoperdon pyriforme is unusual among puffballs in that it grows on tree stumps and other dead wood, often in large clumps. It is pale yellow at first and becomes brown as it ripens. Although ripe in autumn, old skins can be found at any time of the year. About 3 cm across.

Scleroderma citrinum (Common Earthball) appears in summer and autumn, usually on sandy ground. Yellowish at first, it becomes brown and cracked when ripe. The spores escape through the cracks. Up to 10 cm across.

Earth-stars

Earth-stars are simple spheres at first,but the outer skin soon splits into several flaps which usually fold back to form the star. They often curl under at the tips and push the spore chamber up above the dead leaves. The spores escape through a small hole at the top of the papery spore chamber.

Geastrum triplex and **Geastrum striatum** are earth-stars which grow in deciduous woods in the autumn. The chamber of *triplex* is about 3 cm across; that of *striatum* is only 1 cm across.

Bird's-nest Fungi

When ripe, bird's-nest fungi have fruiting bodies which resemble little nests with eggs in. The spores develop inside the 'eggs'. Raindrops splash out the 'eggs' which then split open to allow the spores to escape.

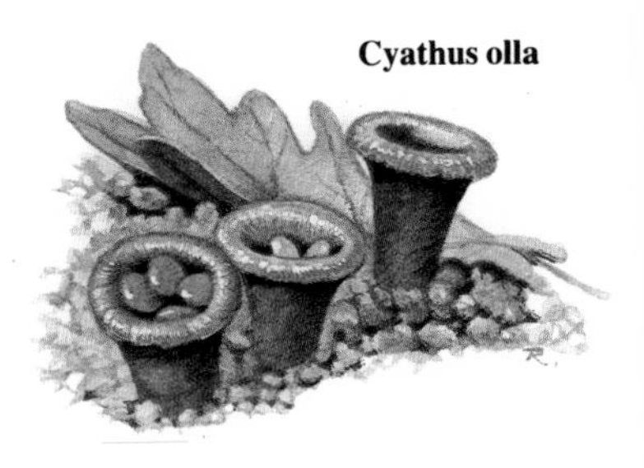

Cyathus olla

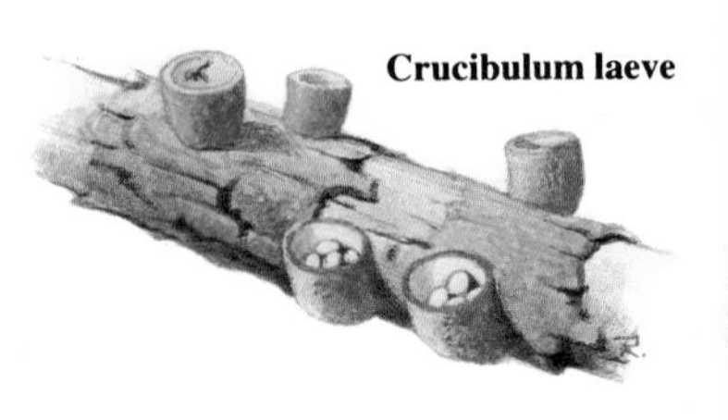

Crucibulum laeve

Cyathus olla grows on the ground in woods and hedgerows at most times of the year. About 1 cm across.

Crucibulum laeve grows on dead twigs in autumn and winter. It is only about 5 mm across.

Geastrum striatum

Geastrum triplex

Bracket Fungi

Bracket fungi grow on trees. Their fruiting bodies are shaped like brackets or shelves. Nearly all belong to the group known as polypores. The lower surface of the bracket bears thousands of tiny pores like those found in the boletes (page 28). The flesh is often tough and woody. Bracket fungi usually attack dead trunks and branches, but some attack living trees and may actually kill them.

Polyporus squamosus (Dryad's Saddle) is especially common on elm, but grows on many other deciduous trees. The brackets often grow in overlapping tiers and may be high up on the trunk. They can be seen from April to December, but they are quite soft and each bracket lasts for only a few months. The fungus weakens the trees and often causes the branches to snap off. Up to 60 cm across.

Griffolia frondosa forms dense tufts of fan-shaped brackets. They are greyish or pale brown above and dirty white below, with a white, stem-like base. The pores are of

Polyporus squamosus

Griffolia frondosa

irregular size. The fungus has a strong, mouse-like smell. It appears in the summer and autumn on stumps and bases of broad-leaved trees and is particularly common on oak. About 6 cm across.

Ganoderma applanatum can be found on various trees all the year. It is especially common on beech and often kills this tree. The tough brackets often grow in tiers. The upper surface is distinctly wavy. The margin is white when young but becomes darker later. The brown spores resemble cocoa powder. Up to 40 cm across.

Fomes fomentarius produces bracket-shaped or hoof-like fruiting bodies which are greyish above and pale brown below. They are very hard and can be seen at all times of year. The fungus grows mainly on birch and beech. Up to 50 cm across.

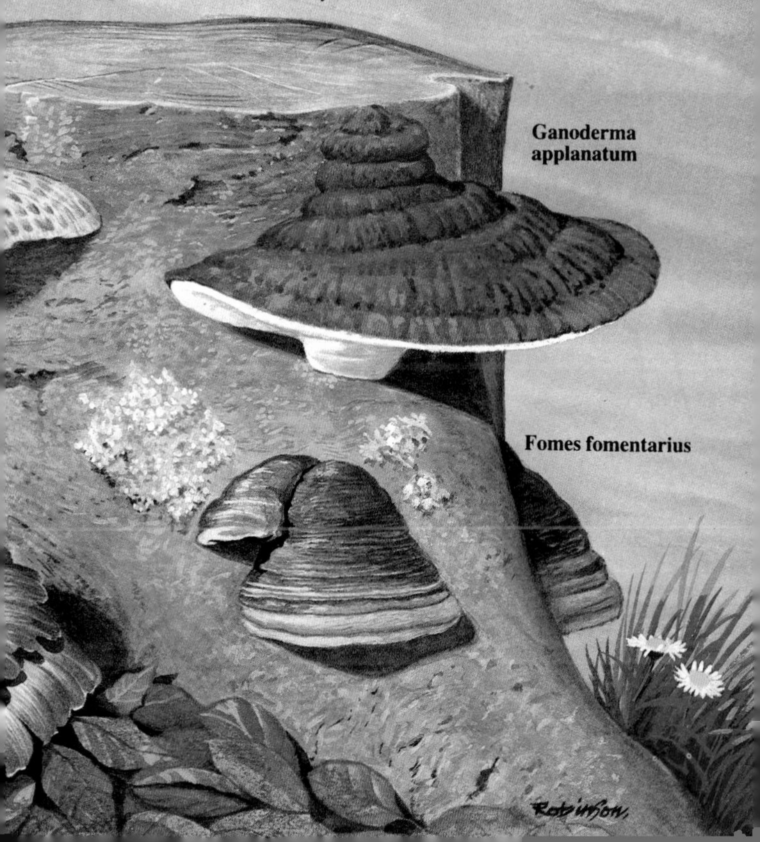

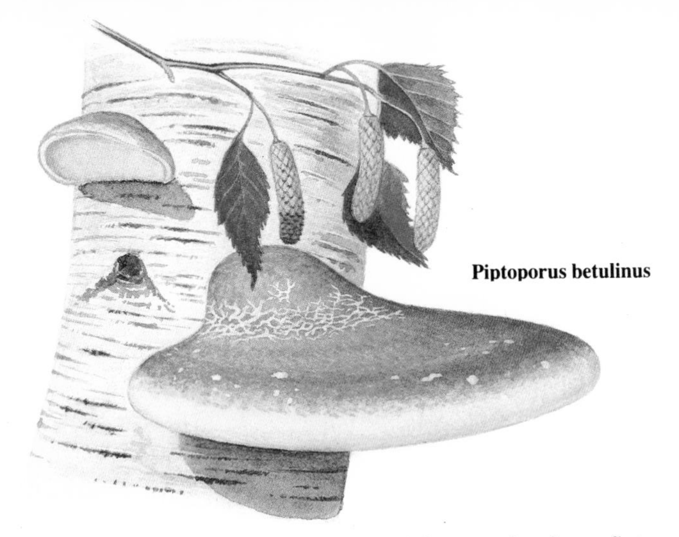
Piptoporus betulinus

Piptoporus betulinus (**Birch Bracket**) can be found on birch trees throughout the year. The brackets are rather hoof-shaped and have a corky texture. The fungus attacks living trunks and often kills them. It then goes on growing on the dead wood, causing it to decay rapidly. About 15 cm across.

Daedalea quercina forms flat brackets on dead stumps – mainly oaks. The brackets have a distinctly grooved surface. The pores are elongate and irregular, giving the lower surface a maze-like appearance. The brackets are tough and woody and can be found at all times of the year. Up to 30 cm across.

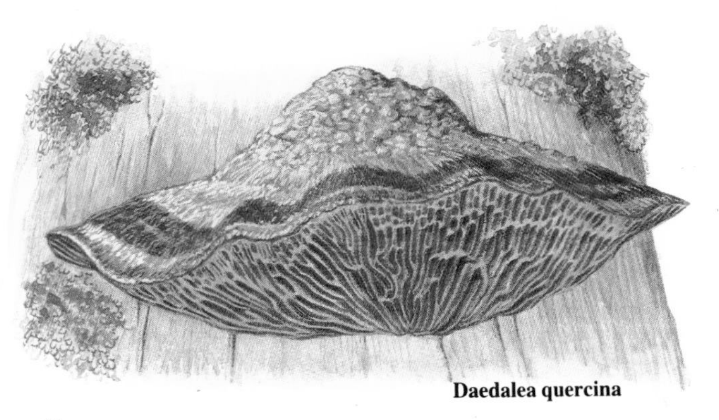
Daedalea quercina

Fistulina hepatica (**Beefsteak Fungus**) has flesh the colour and texture of raw beef. It also 'bleeds' when damaged. It grows mainly on stumps and trunks of oak. The fan-shaped or hoof-like bracket has a yellowish underside. The small pores do not touch each other. The brackets, which grow singly, appear in late summer and autumn and do not last more than a few weeks. Up to 15 cm across.

Daedaleopsis confragosa can be found all year, mainly on slender trunks and branches of willows. The underside is dirty white, often turning red if bruised, and the pores are long and narrow. Up to 15 cm across.

Coriolus versicolor is common on stumps and fallen branches, often in dense tiers. The brackets are thin and leathery, with a felty surface. They can be found at any time, although individual brackets are not long-lived. The pores are very small. Up to 8 cm across.

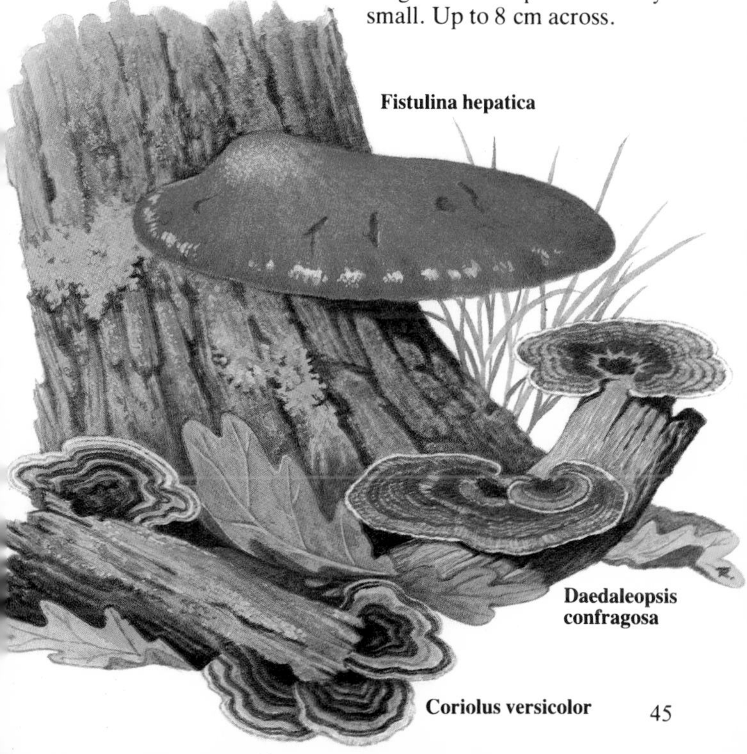

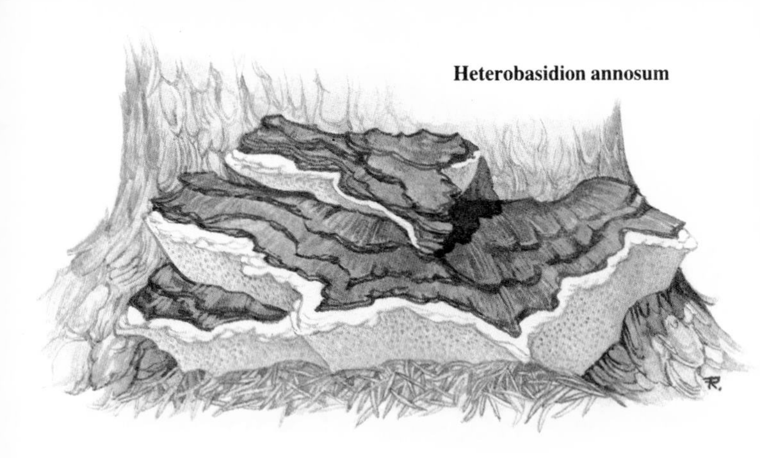

Heterobasidion annosum

Heterobasidion annosum grows mainly on coniferous trees and kills large numbers of them. The brackets usually spring from the roots or the base of the trunk, but sometimes appear on dead stumps. They are very hard and woody with a knobbly surface and a thin white margin. The underside is cream. The fungus can be seen at all times of the year. Up to 20 cm across.

Hymenochaete rubiginosa is not one of the polypores because it has no pores on the underside, but it forms very definite brackets on stumps and fallen branches of deciduous trees, especially oaks. The brackets are thin and velvety and rather brittle. Spores are produced all over the waxy brown underside, but the spores themselves are white. The brackets can be found all through the year. Up to 7 cm across.

Hymenochaete rubiginosa

Bjerkandera adusta

Bjerkandera adusta produces flexible leathery brackets on a range of deciduous trees – usually on the dead trunks. The brackets are often densely tiered and may cover a large area. Both surfaces are usually smoky grey, with a white margin when young. Up to 7 cm across.

Pleurotus ostreatus (**Oyster Fungus**) grows in tiers on trunks and dead stumps of deciduous trees, especially beech. It appears mainly in autumn. It is an agaric, with gills under the cap. There is sometimes a short stalk at one side. The cap is up to 12 cm across.

Pleurotus ostreatus

Odd-shaped Fungi

The fungi illustrated on the next six pages produce a wide variety of fruiting bodies but none exhibits the umbrella shape of the typical mushroom or toadstool. They have neither gills nor pores, and the spores are produced on various parts of the surface. The species illustrated on these two pages all belong to the major group known as the Ascomycetes, in which the spores are formed inside cells called asci (see page 7). The asci themselves are scattered over or embedded in certain areas of the surface of the fruiting body.

Daldinia concentrica (**King Alfred's Cakes**) can be found throughout the year on dead trunks and branches, especially those of ash trees. Like small burnt buns, they are dark brown when young and black and very hard when mature. Millions of soot-like spores are released from the surface. If cut open they reveal a layered structure of light and dark zones. Up to 6 cm across: sometimes larger.

Daldinia concentrica

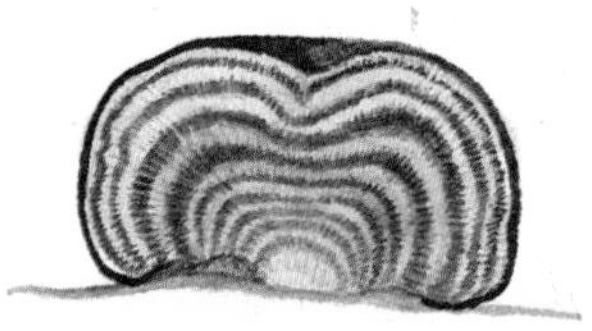

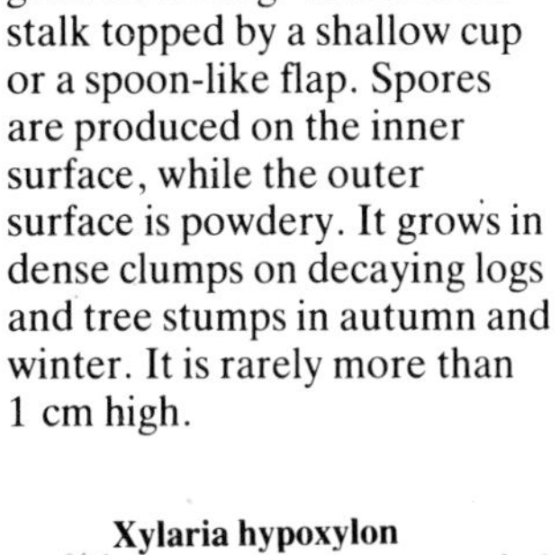

Coryne sarcoides is a bright gelatinous fungi with a short stalk topped by a shallow cup or a spoon-like flap. Spores are produced on the inner surface, while the outer surface is powdery. It grows in dense clumps on decaying logs and tree stumps in autumn and winter. It is rarely more than 1 cm high.

Coryne sarcoides

Xylaria hypoxylon

Xylaria hypoxylon (Candle Snuff) can be found at all times of the year on tree stumps and other dead wood. The leathery, strap-like stalks are very tough and usually forked. Powdery white spores develop near the tips of young stalks, but the true ascospores are black and are produced near the base. Height: 2–3 cm.

Nectria cinnabarina (Coral Spot) is well-known to gardeners, for it rapidly destroys pea sticks and other dead twigs. The threads grow through the twigs and produce two different kinds of spore-bearing cushions on the surface. The commonest of these are the little pink spots which give the fungus its name. The other kind of cushion is dark red. Grows throughout the year.

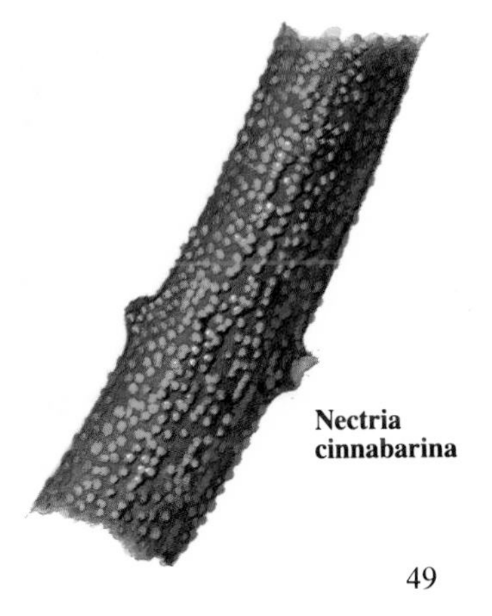

Nectria cinnabarina

Helvella lacunosa is an ascomycete which grows in deciduous woods, often springing up from burnt ground. The deeply-grooved stalk is hollow and bears two irregular lobes which bear the spores. Autumn. Height: up to 10 cm.

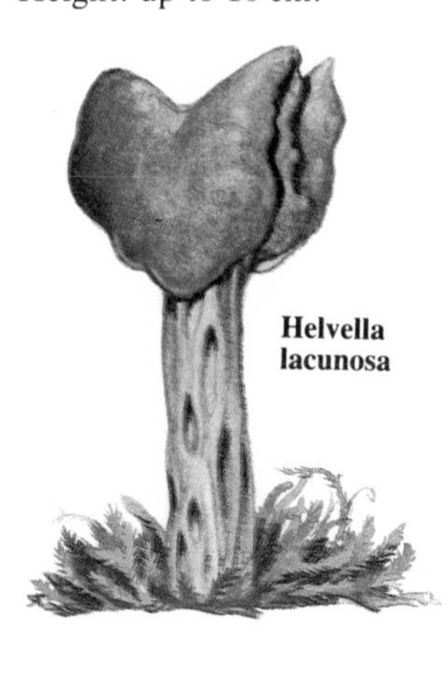

Helvella lacunosa

Cup Fungi

Cup Fungi are ascomycetes, closely related to *Helvella*. The fruiting body is a shallow cup-shaped disc,often brightly coloured, with the asci scattered over the upper surface. Most species are small and all are rather brittle. The majority live on the ground, although some grow on dead wood.

Peziza succosa is a cup fungus which grows on bare soil, especially in woods, in the summer. It is common but, being dull brown, is easily overlooked. It sometimes has a violet tinge. It exudes a yellowish juice if crushed. Up to 4 cm across.

Peziza coccinea grows on rotting wood and is found mainly in winter. The cup is borne on a short stalk. Up to 6 cm across.

Peziza succosa

Peziza coccinea

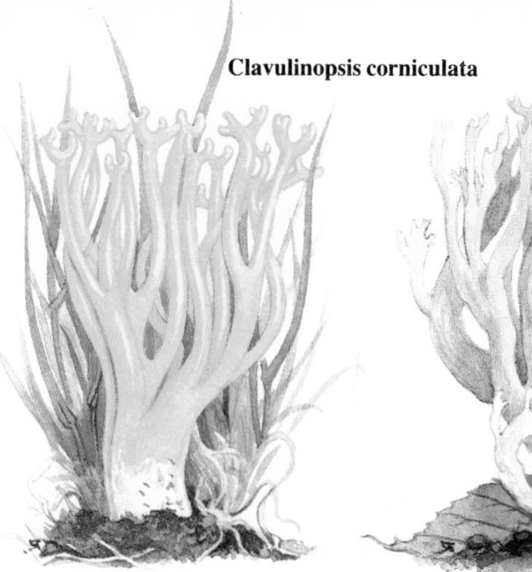
Clavulinopsis corniculata

Clavulina cinerea

Peziza aurantia (Orange-Peel Fungus) is a familiar cup fungus of footpaths and other bare or well-trodden ground. The bright orange upper side and downy white lower surface give it just the appearance of orange peel. Autumn and winter. Up to 12 cm across.

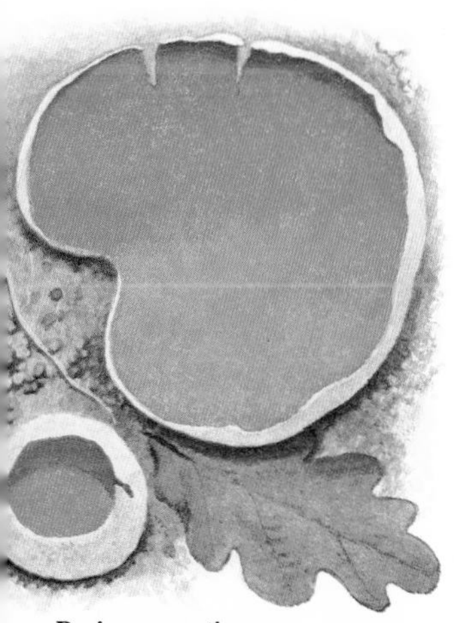
Peziza aurantia

Basidiomycetes

The fungi illustrated above and on the following two pages are all basidiomycetes, in which the spores are borne on the outside of cells called basidia (see page 7).

Clavulina cinerea is one of the coral fungi. The fruiting body is irregularly branched like a grey coral and grows on the ground in dense clusters, usually in deciduous woods. Autumn. Height: up to 9 cm.

Clavulinopsis corniculata is a coral fungus. It might be mistaken for *Calocera viscosa* (page 52) but the tough texture and forked or horse-shoe-shaped tips readily distinguish it. It grows on the ground, mainly in woods, in autumn. Height: up to 7 cm.

Auricularia auricula-judae

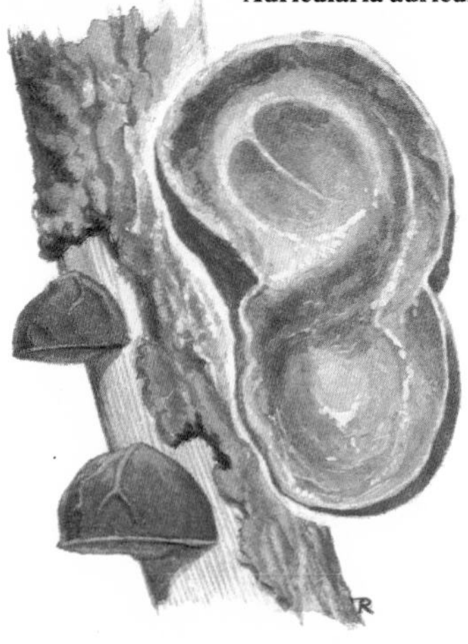

Auricularia auricula-judae (Jew's Ear) is one of a group known as jelly fungi. The fruiting body is remarkably like an ear, with a rubbery texture and a velvety surface. It is gelatinous when wet. Spores develop all over the inner surface. It grows on elder trees and can be found throughout the year. Up to 10 cm across.

Calocera viscosa is another jelly fungus, whose antler-like stalks are soft and slimy when damp but horny when dry. It grows on conifer stumps from autumn to spring. Up to 8 cm high.

Tremella mesenterica is a third jelly fungus, growing on dead trunks and branches throughout the year but especially common in autumn and winter. The fruiting body becomes hard when dry. Up to 10 cm across.

Serpula lachrymans (Dry Rot) is a serious pest in old, damp buildings, where it attacks floor boards and other concealed timbers. The wood becomes clothed with a

Calocera viscosa

Tremella mesenterica

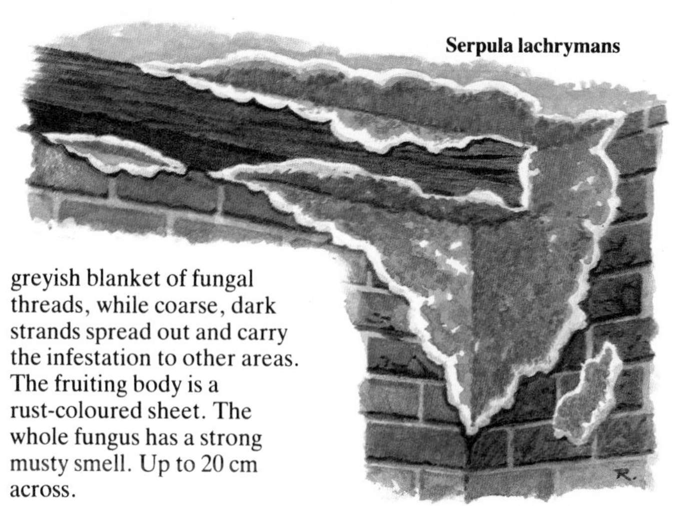
Serpula lachrymans

greyish blanket of fungal threads, while coarse, dark strands spread out and carry the infestation to other areas. The fruiting body is a rust-coloured sheet. The whole fungus has a strong musty smell. Up to 20 cm across.

Sparassis crispa (**Cauliflower Fungus**) forms pale, cauliflower-like masses at the base of conifer trunks in autumn. Each 'cauliflower' consists of a mass of short, brittle branches which are clothed with spores. Up to 30 cm across.

Thelophora terrestris forms soft, felt-like rosettes on the ground in coniferous woods and on heathland. Up to 6 cm across, each rosette is fan-shaped or funnel-shaped with a fringed margin. Autumn.

Thelophora terrestris

Sparassis crispa

Lichens

Lichens are very unusual plants, each consisting of an intricate mixture of a fungus and many tiny green plants called algae. The fungi in these partnerships cannot grow without their food-providing algal partners. Most lichens are extremely hardy and many grow on bare rocks in very hot or very cold places. Growth is slow and the plants are long-lived. Some form granular crusts on rocks and tree trunks; some form rosettes of more or less flat, branching lobes; others are like tiny bushes. Spores come from the fungus partner only, but they cannot grow unless they find the right alga. Lichens also reproduce by scattering tiny flakes from the surface. These contain both fungus and alga.

Xanthoria parietina forms rosettes on trees, rocks, and walls, especially near the sea. Spores are formed in shallow orange cups near the centre.

Ramalina siliquosa (Sea Ivory) forms tufts of flat branches on coastal rocks just above high tide level. Spores are borne on flat discs at the tips of the branches.

Ramalina calicaris forms tufts on trees. Each branch has a groove running along it. The spores develop on pale discs scattered over the branches.

Hypogymnia physodes forms rosettes on old tree trunks. The underside is firmly

Xanthoria parietina

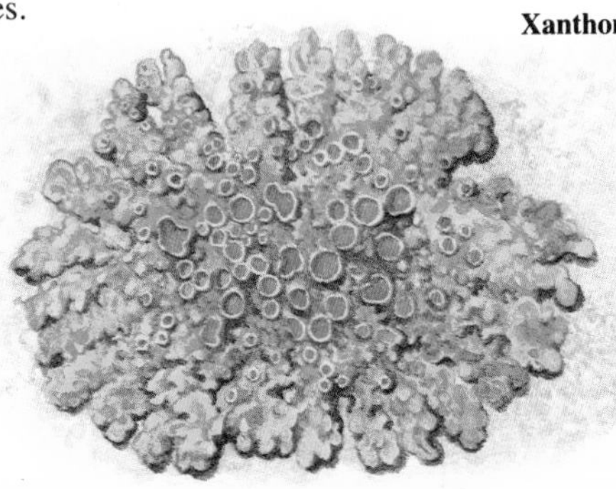

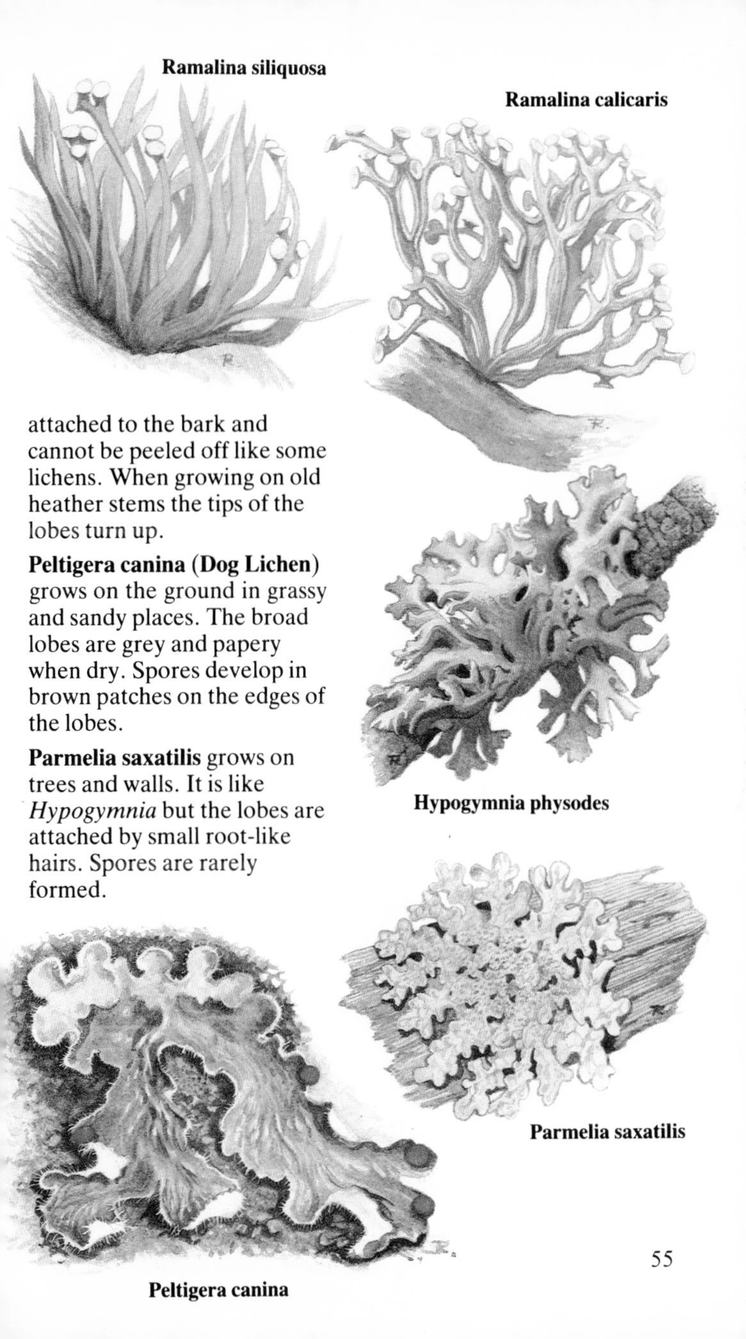

attached to the bark and cannot be peeled off like some lichens. When growing on old heather stems the tips of the lobes turn up.

Peltigera canina (**Dog Lichen**) grows on the ground in grassy and sandy places. The broad lobes are grey and papery when dry. Spores develop in brown patches on the edges of the lobes.

Parmelia saxatilis grows on trees and walls. It is like *Hypogymnia* but the lobes are attached by small root-like hairs. Spores are rarely formed.

Ochrolechia parella

Cladonia rangiformis

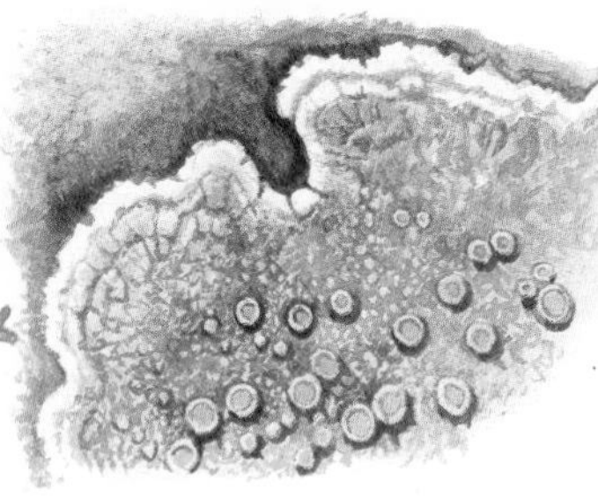

Ochrolechia parella is common on rocks and walls, forming a rough crust. Spores are borne in pinkish-brown discs.

Cladonia rangiformis forms bushy clumps of forked stems on heathland and sand dunes. Spores develop in small patches on the stems.

Cladonia fimbriata (Pixie Cup) grows on walls, tree stumps, and the ground.

Cladonia floerkeana and **Cladonia coccifera** both grow on heaths and moorland. The stalks spring from cushions of scales. Spores develop in the red patches.

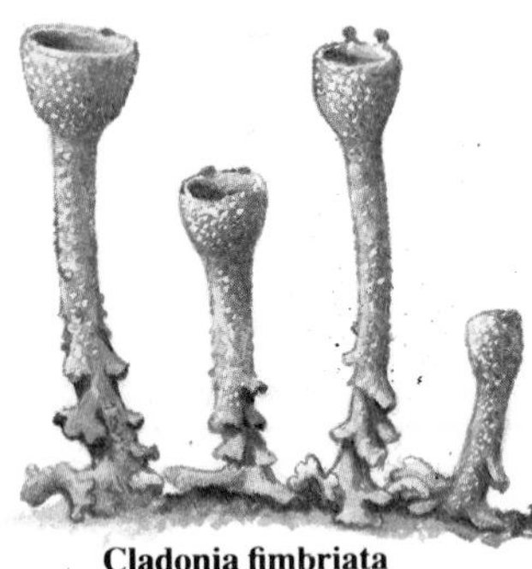

Cladonia fimbriata

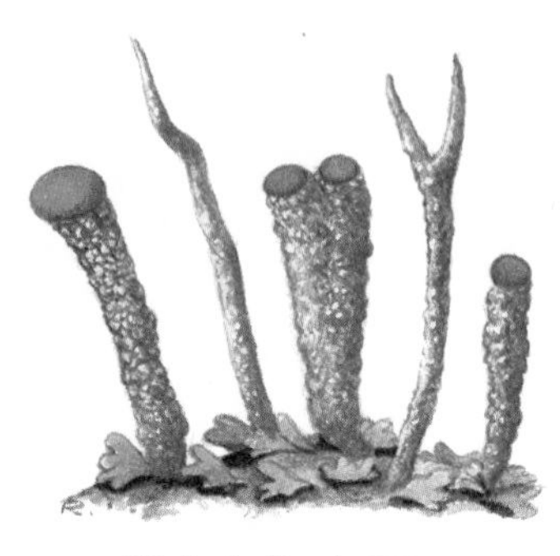

Cladonia floerkeana

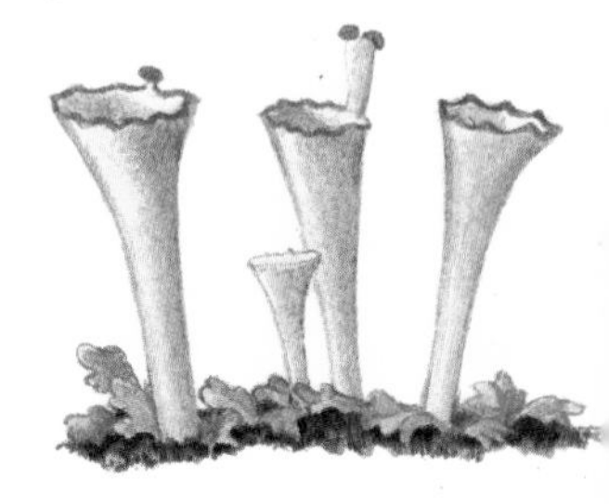

Cladonia coccifera

Lecanora muralis

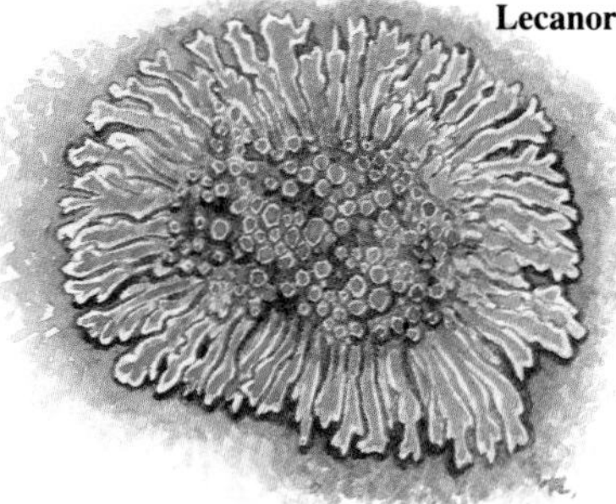

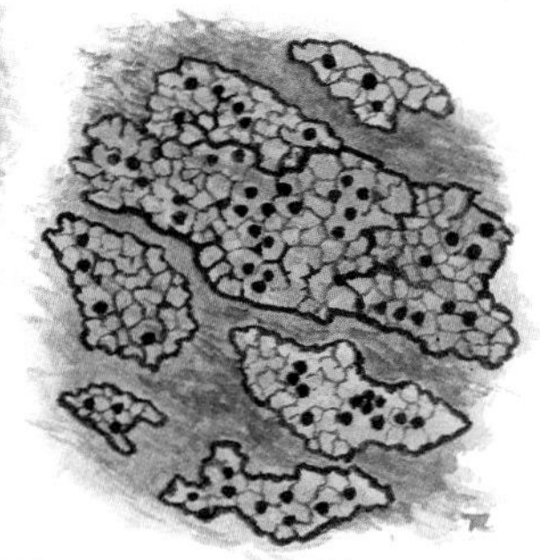

Rhizocarpon geographicum

Lecanora muralis is a crusty lichen but has a marginal ring of pale lobes. It is abundant on rocks and walls. Spores develop in brown discs.

Rhizocarpon geographicum (**Map Lichen**) has a thin black margin to its crust. It grows on rocks and the margins meet like map boundaries.

Graphis elegans forms thin crusts on tree trunks. The black spore-bearing areas look like writing, hence its name.

Usnea florida and **Usnea subfloridans** are beard lichens, forming tangled tufts on tree trunks in damp climates.

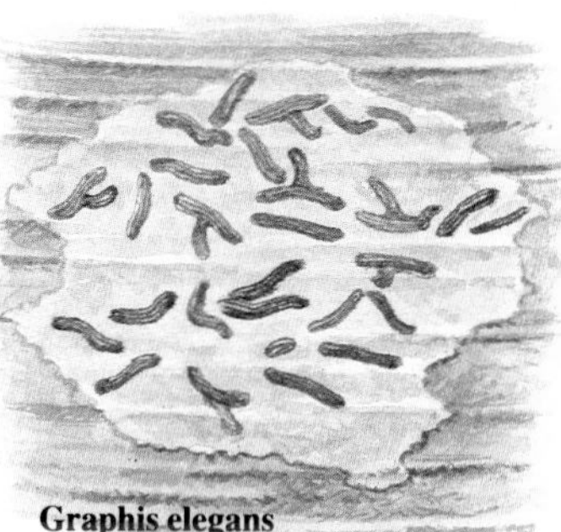

Graphis elegans

Usnea florida

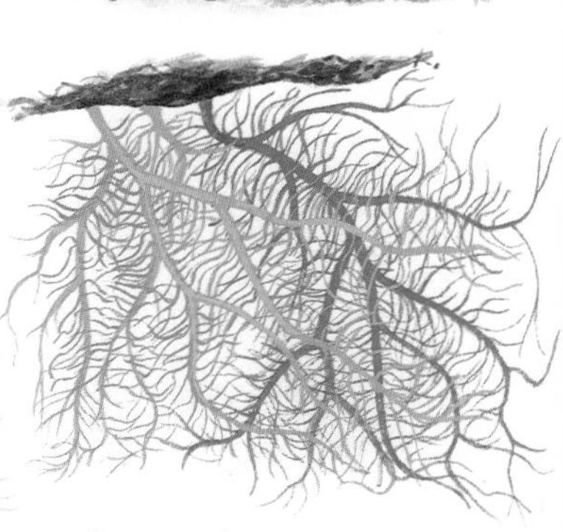

Usnea subfloridans

Some Common Moulds

Moulds are fungi whose threads form dense and often fluffy mats (mycelia) over their food materials. Most of them live in very damp places. Many of them damage our foods, including bread, fruit, and jam; others cause disease in our crops. However, some moulds are very useful, for example, *Penicillium* moulds produce penicillin, the antibiotic which is used in medicine to fight germs

Moulds do not produce elaborate fruiting bodies, although there may be special areas of spore-bearing hyphae. Many moulds belong to the large group known as the Lower Fungi (Phycomycetes), which differ from the larger kinds in having no partition in their threads. Many more are ascomycetes. Most of them produce several kinds of spores.

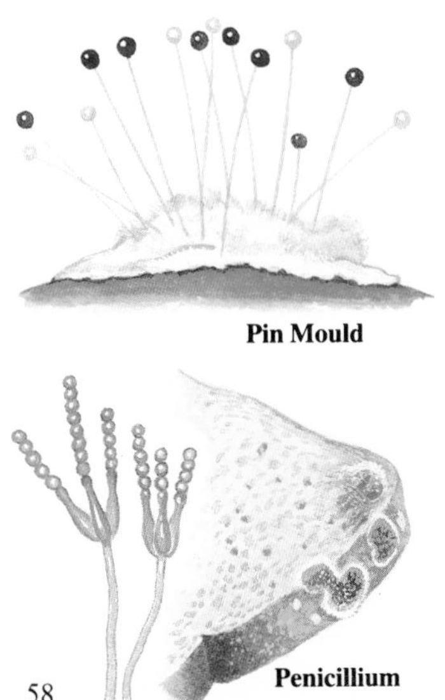

Pin Mould

Penicillium

Pin Moulds (Mucor), of which there are several similar kinds, are so named because their spore capsules, raised on slender stalks, resemble tiny pins. The fluffy mycelium grows on dung, as well as bread and many other foods. Pin moulds are phycomycetes.

Penicillium moulds form green mats on bread, over-ripe fruit, and many other foods. They can grow in drier places than many other moulds. They are ascomycetes, but asci are rare. Chains of other kinds of spores are formed all over the surface.

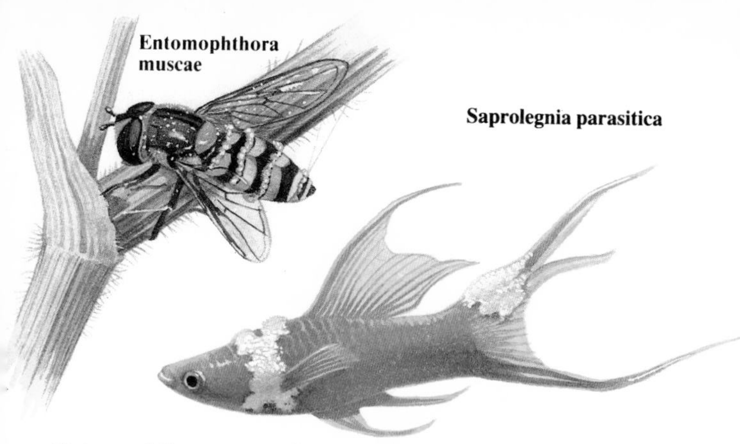

Entomophthora muscae is a phycomycete parasite of house-flies. Threads spread through the fly's body and soon kill it. They break out and form fluffy spore-bearing patches on the surface of the insect. Flies killed by the fungus can be seen stuck to window panes in the autumn.

Saprolegnia paraistica attacks fishes. The fungus enters a wound and its presence is revealed by small tufts of hyphae on the fins or elsewhere. Eventually the fungal threads kill the fish.

Brown apple rot (Sclerotinia fructigena) This fungus invades apples through small wounds and forms large, brown patches. It may develop while the apples are on the tree or after they have been picked. Spores are formed on cottony tufts on the surface and can infect neighbouring apples. Affected apples may become black and hard.

Pilobolus species form glistening spore capsules on cowpats and other dung. The whole spore capsule is fired onto the surrounding grass.

Fungi Causing Plant Diseases

Black Spot on roses is caused by *Diplocarpon rosae*. Black blotches develop on both sides of the leaves, and affected leaves may become yellow and fall. Spores produced on the black patches spread to new leaves. The patches remain on fallen leaves through the winter and the spores then re-infect the bushes in the spring.

Black Spot

Potato Blight, which was responsible for widespread famine in Ireland in the 1840's, is caused by a phycomycete, *Phytophthora infestans*. The fungus infests the whole potato plant and causes the leaves and tubers to rot. It spreads mainly in damp conditions.

Wheat Rust (Puccinia graminis) is a basidiomycete with a complex life history and several kinds of spores – some of which live on barberry leaves. It produces black and rust-coloured patches on wheat leaves.

Potato Blight

Wheat Rust

Ergot

Vine Mildew

Ergot (Claviceps purpurea) is an ascomycete parasite of rye. The grains become replaced by small black banana-shaped objects known as sclerotia. These pass the winter in the soil and produce spores in the spring. The sclerotia are very poisonous.

Vine Mildew (Uncinula necator) is one of the powdery mildews, so called because they cover their host plants with thick deposits of spores. It is an ascomycete.

Club-root of cabbage is caused by *Plasmodiophora brassicae*, which belongs to a strange group of fungi called slime moulds. It causes the roots to swell enormously. They cannot absorb water properly and the leaves become limp and bluish. Adding lime to the soil helps to control the disease.

Silver-leaf disease

Silver-leaf disease in plum trees is caused by the basidiomycete *Stereum purpureum*. The leaves turn silvery and the branches may die. Fruiting bodies in the form of purplish, leathery crusts push though the bark.

Damping-off is a disease which often attacks seedlings which get too wet, causing them to rot at the base. This is as a result of attack by *Pythium* species, which are phycomycetes.

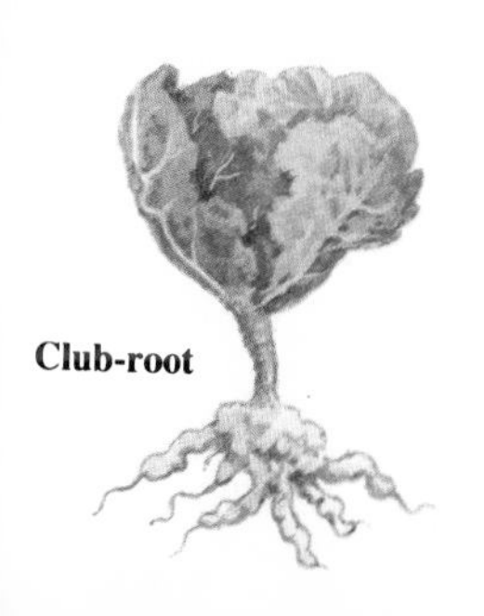

Club-root

Damping-off

Index